THE INCREASE OF HIS GOVERNMENT

THE KINGDOM IS HERE AND IT IS COMING

ADAM LIVECCHI

THE INCREASE OF HIS GOVERNMENT

THE KINGDOM IS HERE AND IT IS COMING

ADAM LIVECCHI

All Scripture taken from the King James Version which is in the Public Domain.

THE INCREASE OF HIS GOVERNMENT

ISBN 978-0-9835523-5-2

©2012 by Adam LiVecchi. All rights reserved. This book is protected by the copyright laws of the United States of America. No part of this publication may be reproduced, stored in a retrieval system, or transmitted in any form or by any means electronic, mechanical, photocopying, recording, or otherwise, without the prior written permission of the publisher or under consentual agreement.

Printed in the United States of America.

First Printing: August 2012

Cover art done by Ryan Smyth, Royal Essex.
www.RoyalEssex.com

For more information on how to order this book or any of the other materials We See Jesus Ministries offers please contact:

We See Jesus Ministries
www.WeSeeJesusMinistries.com

DEDICATION

I dedicate this book to all my brothers and sisters around the world who are suffering and have suffered for the name of Jesus. This is dedicated to Christians who are really like Christ, to those who were, are and will be counted worthy to suffer for His great name. You are the heroes and great is your reward in heaven. More specifically I dedicate this book Brother Yun of China also known as the heavenly man and Pastor Youcef Nadarkhani of Iran. Great is your reward in heaven. (Both of these men were in jail for the witness of the Kingdom in their lives. They are heroes!)

"Confirming the souls of the disciples, and exhorting them to continue in the faith, and that we must through much tribulation enter into the kingdom of God." (Acts 14:22)

SPECIAL THANKS TO

My beloved Sarah you mean the world to me. I enjoy your company, and I appreciate everything you do and say. Sarah you have never said one discouraging word to me. You are so amazing. I hope to learn to love you like Christ loves the church.

I want to take this opportunity to honor my Father Angelo and Mother Andrea LiVecchi for pouring life into me and for helping me in every way. Thank you for having a home with no compromise in it when I was young and impressionable. Seeing Jesus in your family growing up was a great privilege. I love and appreciate you.

My Brother Aaron LiVecchi, your faithfulness and hunger for Jesus is amazing. I am really proud of you for setting your life apart for Jesus and his Kingdom.

Special thanks to Julia Hali for her help with editing this book.

TABLE OF CONTENTS

PREFACE
The Cross is the Drawbridge into the Kingdom..........................15

CHAPTER 1
Kingdom Creativity and God's Sovereignty................................17

CHAPTER 2
Kingdom Worldview..25

CHAPTER 3
Defining or Re-defining the Kingdom...33

CHAPTER 4
The Supremacy of Jesus Christ..49

CHAPTER 5
The Commands of the Kingdom...59

CHAPTER 6
Pray the Kingdom..69

CHAPTER 7
Seek First the Kingdom..81

CHAPTER 8
Preaching and Releasing the Kingdom...87

CHAPTER 9
The Increase of His Government..99

CHAPTER 10
The Great Commandment and the Great Commission..............111

CHAPTER 11
Blessed Are the Poor..119

CHAPTER 12
The Throne of God..129

CHAPTER 13
Allegiance, Alliances and Citizenship........................135

CHAPTER 14
Adoption, Sonship, Inheritance and Kings and Priests.............145

CHAPTER 15
Kingdom Promotion..157

CHAPTER 16
The Attributes of the Kingdom..................................167

FINAL THOUGHTS
Matthew 22..179

PREFACE

THE CROSS IS THE DRAWBRIDGE INTO THE KINGDOM OF GOD

The centrality of all Kingdom teaching must be Christ Jesus. We have no way into the Kingdom without him. Even the thief hanging next to him on Calvary looked at a bleeding naked man hanging from a tree and saw a King. That is why he said, *"Lord remember me in your Kingdom."* He is the only way to the Father. The Lordship of Jesus is the central doctrine of the Kingdom. Anything that you hear about the kingdom of God where Christ isn't mentioned and focused upon just reject it. The most amazing part of the Kingdom is not its grandeur or its abundance but its King. When Jesus was on earth his message was, *"Repent the Kingdom of God is at hand."* As a matter of fact, the purpose of being born again is to see the Kingdom. God has amazing plans for our lives but unless Jesus is truly our Lord both doctrinally and experientially, we will not walk in the fullness of what he has paid for through his shed blood.

If someone is going to be born again, first he or she must die. We first must be crucified with Christ before we are born again. In the Kingdom, we must die to truly live and humble ourselves to be exalted.

"I am crucified with Christ: nevertheless I live; yet not I, but Christ liveth in me: and the life which I now live in the flesh I live by the faith of the Son of God, who loved me, and gave himself for me." (Galatians 2:20)

A kingdom life is Christ the King living his life through us. The revelation of his death must become personal to us. He puts his grace towards us so we can put our faith in him. When we truly rely on and trust in what he has done on the hill of Golgotha, we become dead to sin and alive to him. When we die, we are then born again and ready to see the Kingdom.

"Jesus answered and said unto him, Verily, verily, I say unto thee, Except a man be born again, he cannot see the kingdom of God." (John 3:3)

We are new creations and now we are ready for the Kingdom. When the life of God is inside you, you are living in the Kingdom, and the kingdom is living within you.

The price of the Kingdom was the cross. Jesus paid for our redemption; we are redeemed from sin and death unto life everlasting in the Kingdom of God. The price of the Kingdom was so costly only King Jesus could pay it for us. Everything that will be spoken about in this book is strictly on the merit of the shed blood of Jesus Christ. The blood Christ paid for all that is ours in the Kingdom of God. God gave his Son, and we receive him and his Kingdom. The supremacy of Jesus Christ is the central message of the Kingdom.

CHAPTER 1
CREATIVITY AND SOVEREIGNTY IN THE KINGDOM OF GOD

We are created in the image of the creator, meaning we are very creative by nature because we were created in his likeness. Even the most uncreative person is actually very creative; it's just who we are. We only are who we are because he has created us to be in fellowship with him. Through Jesus alone this is possible; he is the only way to the Father. God's sovereignty and creativity do not conflict with one another. He is sovereign enough to give us a free will. His sovereignty is greater than our free will. That doesn't mean we don't have free will; it means his will can invade this planet at any time or moment and no one can stop him. He is God; he does what he pleases and there is no other. God's sovereignty creates a hunger in us for certainty or truth. It creates a hunger for absolutes. His creativity causes us to desire spontaneity and change, purpose in motion with not all the road map directions before we start the journey. The more we get to know God according to his word and by his Holy Spirit, the clearer who he are and what he desires from us becomes. In God's sovereignty we have choices his wisdom is unsearchable. As he commands us to do something, his authority can flow through our submission. His authority has creativity in it.

> *"And God said, Let us make man in our image, after our likeness: and let them have dominion over the fish of the sea, and over the fowl of the air, and over the cattle, and over all the earth, and over every creeping thing that creepeth upon the earth. So God created man in his own image, in the image of God created he him; male and female created he them. And God blessed them, and God said unto them, Be fruitful, and multiply, and replenish the earth, and subdue it: and have dominion over the fish of the sea, and over the fowl of the air, and over every living thing that moveth upon the earth."*
> (Genesis 1:26-28)

God gave them dominion not Adam. They both were the highest created order on the planet. They had dominion given to them. The dominion was to fulfill a plan. I call the plan, "operation be fruitful multiply and subdue." The church needs to hear this. Muslims are having kids like they are free to raise, while most church people are having a few kids. If the church doesn't wake up, Radical muslims won't have to kill Christians; they will just out populate Christians like 7 or 8 to 1 until we are the minority on the planet. Muslims want to subdue the world while most Christians just want to fill their churches and then go to heaven. We need to wake up and remember the very first thing God said to humans, be fruitful multiply and subdue the earth. In obedience to what God has said we have access to his resources, authority, creativity and power.

If we want access to our inheritance, we must move forward with Jesus. We have to stop looking to the past to define the future. We need what Jesus has said about the future in the Bible to lead us with wisdom and understanding into tomorrow. If we are going to seek first the kingdom of God and his righteousness, we cannot worry about tomorrow. However, we can't neglect making the right choices today. When we live with a Biblical understanding of urgency, it causes us to live faithfully with what God has entrusted us with today. I believe that you desire to be faithful to God and so I am writing about his sovereignty and creativity because I know you are hungry for what God has for you. It's his pleasure to reveal himself; it's his good pleasure to give you the kingdom. Jesus delights to delegate authority to us so that we live in submission to his mission. God is not a control freak. God is not an insecure leader or pastor. When someone wants to control your life more than God run for your life because if you don't you will be in a spider web of religion and control that will be very hard to get out of. They might call it kingdom but it's really not. When authority is used to control people and not release them, something is terribly wrong. God uses his authority to release creativity in the midst of our assignment. This is his sovereignty in motion. Things that are very deep to us are really simple to him. In the simplest of terms, God really trusts you!

> *"And the LORD God said, It is not good that the man should be alone; I will make him an help meet for him. And out of the ground the LORD God formed every beast of the field, and every fowl of the air; and brought them unto Adam to see what he would call them: and whatsoever Adam called every living creature, that was the name thereof. And Adam gave names to all cattle, and to the fowl of the air, and to every beast of the field; but for Adam there was not found an help meet for him. And the LORD God caused a deep sleep to fall upon Adam, and he slept: and he took one of his ribs, and closed up the flesh instead thereof; And the rib, which the LORD God had taken from man, made he a woman, and brought her unto the man. And Adam said, This is now bone of my bones, and flesh of my flesh: she shall be called Woman, because she was taken out of Man."* (Genesis 2:18-23)

God didn't ask Adam if he wanted a wife or if he could borrow one of Adam's ribs. He just said it's not good that Adam or man is alone. God took a rib without asking Adam and made Eve. That is a great picture of God's sovereignty. Before God performed this amazing miracle, he commanded Adam to name the animals. So God brings the animals to Adam so he can name them. At this point Adam has never done anything before. He has no experience naming anything. However, when God commanded him to do it, he became equipped to do that which God had commanded. We are equipped by the command of the Lord. When we set it in our heart to obey, he releases *grace in the time of need* so we can get the job done.

"Let us therefore come boldly unto the throne of grace, that we may obtain mercy, and find grace to help in time of need." (Hebrews 4:16)

Grace is released in the time of need, and it helps to accomplish something both in us and through us.

God didn't give Adam a checklist with the pictures of the animas and their names. He brought the animals to him and trusted that he would do a good job. This was Adam's only real accomplishment before sin entered into the world. In the historical account of creation and eventually the fall of mankind we can learn many things. The thing that I am most interested in is, what is God like? Who is he? What is he doing? That is my deepest interest. God knew Adam was going to name a lamb, a lamb. Jesus was the Lamb slain before the foundation of the world according to Revelation 13:8. If Adam didn't name a lamb a lamb, we would have some serious problems. It was God's very breath in Adam that named the animals anyway. In God's equation there is his sovereignty and creativity, his love and his wrath, his judgment and his mercy. The very animal Adam named Jesus later would come down and clothe him with to cover his nakedness. He is the creator; he's also a fashion designer who designed the first leather garments on the planet, see Genesis 3:22. Jesus is a creator, designer and King; it's just who he is. Our King rules and creates by speaking. His Sovereignty and creativity help us to accomplish his will. God's sovereignty delegates authority to us so we can fulfill what he desires. There are certain things that God won't micro manage in our life the same way that God didn't name the animals for Adam. He in his sovereignty has given us creativity to choose, and so we must choose wisely. Wisdom is necessary in all of our choices. When Jesus gives us a command, our only choice should be to obey especially if we call Jesus Lord. *Radical obedience is the simplest definition of a Kingdom lifestyle.* However, when he doesn't give a command about something specific we need to use wisdom. Wisdom is the facilitator of purpose, destiny and success. Anything good that is sustainable must have wisdom; wisdom is the sustainer of power. For example, power lines must be covered in rubber. The rubber that protects the power flow is a picture of how wisdom facilitates and makes power sustainable. All that power will be gone if it doesn't have a sustainable weatherproof structure around it. There is no compromise in the wisdom that comes from the mouth of the Lord Jesus Christ. Spiritual wisdom is never devoid of truth; wisdom is the proper application of truth. Wisdom was for Adam to obey God and to name the animals God created. When Adam chose to obey, he had access to creativity. Adam gave them names that defined their God given purpose in the created order. Here God's sovereignty and Adam's creativity are flowing together. Creativity was naming animals when they had no names. Creativity creates something out of nothing. When we choose to obey God we have access to his authority and creativity so we can accomplish that which he has commanded us to do.

We will see the concept of God's sovereignty and human creativity working together in the New Testament also. *I am not making any kind of doctrine or authoritative statement.* I am just showing what God has done and through that we can recognize him in motion in our lives. There are things that people are waiting on God for and he's actually waiting on us.

"It is the glory of God to conceal a thing: but the honor of kings is to search out a matter." (Proverbs 25:2)

This is an example of God hiding something from us that is for us if we will only ask, seek and knock. Bill Johnson said it like this "God doesn't hid things from us he hides things for us." We must search if we expect him to reveal. Waiting is the time in which he reveals that which we are looking for. He's not going to reveal it unless we search for it. In our searching he reveals. So many people in life don't know what season they are in and they are waiting when they should be seeking. While we seek, we wait for him to reveal. Perseverance is patience in motion. It's like the writer of Hebrews who says, *"Let us run with patience looking unto Jesus."* He graces us to endure but we have to run. When people can recognize what God is doing, it becomes easier to partner with him. We must never hold God responsible for our part of the equation. We must also learn not to blame God for something satan has done. As sons and daughter of the Kingdom, we must understand our responsibilities and our inheritance. We must never try to earn something God has already given freely. Remember there are no orphans in the Kingdom. We must use wisdom and never sell or squander what we have received freely by God's grace.

Adam named the animals and the Apostles rolled the dice. I am NOT affirming gambling or any other sinful behavior. We are simply going to see God's sovereignty at work even in man's creativity.

> *"For it is written in the book of Psalms, Let his habitation be desolate, and let no man dwell therein: and his bishoprick let another take. Wherefore of these men which have companied with us all the time that the Lord Jesus went in and out among us, Beginning from the baptism of John, unto that same day that he was taken up from us, must one be ordained to be a witness with us of his resurrection. And they appointed two, Joseph called Barsabas, who was surnamed Justus, and Matthias. And they prayed, and said, Thou, Lord, which knowest the hearts of all men, show whether of these two thou hast chosen, That he may take part of this ministry and apostleship, from which Judas by transgression fell, that he might go to his own place. And they gave forth their lots; and the lot fell upon Matthias; and he was numbered with the eleven apostles." (Acts 1:20-26)*

The apostles knew there were requirements for selecting someone to be the 12th Apostle. However, they didn't know who, and they didn't tell us that the Lord outright told them who. They prayed and cast lots, which is similar to rolling dice in our culture today. The apostles trusted God to have the lot fall on the man who was God's choice. In their creativity, they trusted God's sovereignty and invited it into the circumstances by prayer.

Lets see the eternal ramifications of this creative decision. Revelation 21:14 says, *"And the wall of the city had twelve foundations, and in them the names of the twelve apostles of the Lamb."* In the city of God there is a wall, and it has twelve foundations and in the foundations are the names of the twelve apostles. One of their names got there in a pretty interesting and creative way. Through one little game someone's name is eternally written in New Jerusalem the city of God where Jesus himself is the light. Not bad for the roll of a die or the casting of a lot, that sure kicks the lottery in the pants. One of the ways God builds is through creativity. Creativity is one of the things that clearly draws a line between the developing world and the developed world. Everything in the developed world began with an idea. In the developing world the ideas are still to be developed. The developing world is not fully developed because of corruption and all kinds of other evil that humans do to one another. The reality still stands that before something is created it is first an idea. Ideas are how creativity can become reality if they are acted upon.

I have a dear friend who God has graced to be an inventor. I call that kingdom creativity. I personally believe that God wants to release creativity more and more to the body of Christ. This gift is given to those who give their ears to hear what the Holy Spirit is saying to the church.

"I wisdom dwell with prudence, and find out knowledge of witty inventions." (Proverbs 8:12)

Wisdom and prudence are kingdom attributes and when they come together knowledge for creativity is released. A witty invention is something that did not exist before wisdom and prudence came together. A Kingdom life is a life filled with virtues that flow from the King as we live in submission to him. When we submit to his Lordship, his virtues grow in our life and we bear fruit in and out of season. We as believers really need to believe if we are going to operate in our Kingdom inheritance. The blood of our King on Calvary paid for this inheritance to be ours, and we must receive it by faith and not try to earn it by works. Biblical faith empowers us to work. Our faith is not proven by our works, our works only make our faith visible.

"For we are his workmanship, created in Christ Jesus unto good works, which God hath before ordained that we should walk in them." (Ephesians 2:10)

In the kingdom, there is room for you and there is a work for you to do. You were actually created to be someone and do something; you were created to know God. You were not just created to be a tithing, bench warming church attendee. God has created you uniquely to accomplish something amazing that will cause you to know him and people to see Jesus through your life as you obey him. The ultimate privilege in the Kingdom is to know Jesus and the ultimate responsibility is to properly represent him on earth.

CHAPTER 2

KINGDOM WORLDVIEW

A kingdom worldview is necessary if we are going to live in the world and not be of the world. False doctrine doesn't just come from missing two of our daily devotional times in one month. False doctrine fits inside a bigger problem. When you have a Biblical Kingdom worldview, false doctrine can be discerned. However, if someone has a bad worldview like perhaps a secular worldview often times false doctrine goes unnoticed. If our worldview were a wineskin then the new wine would be our doctrine. *That is not what the Bible talks about when it mentions a wineskin or new wine; I am merely using it as an analogy to make this point visible.* **In the Kingdom of God there are no false doctrines or seducing spirits.** Everything in the Kingdom of God is under Jesus' complete leadership. Jesus said that the Father is greater than I, the only thing that the Father knows that Jesus doesn't is the time of Jesus' return.

"But of that day and hour knoweth no man, no, not the angels of heaven, but my Father only. But as the days of Noah were, so shall also the coming of the Son of man be." (Matthew 24:36-37)

That **maybe** why Jesus said the Father is greater than I. That's only a guess, don't make a doctrine out of it and don't put me on a heresy website because of what I just said.

During the New Testament, there were two predominate worldviews. I am going to briefly mention both of them.

"For the Jews require a sign, and the Greeks seek after wisdom: But we preach Christ crucified, unto the Jews a stumblingblock, and unto the Greeks foolishness; But unto them which are called, both Jews and Greeks, Christ the power of God, and the wisdom of God."
(1 Corinthians 1:22-24)

The Jews had a worldview that valued and sought after power and the Greeks had a worldview that valued and sought after wisdom. Both wisdom and power are consummated in Christ Jesus; he was what they were both looking for. Worldview is about a person and not necessarily only a perception. Christians have been given the mind of Christ, so we have a correct worldview. We need to see the world through the eyes of Jesus. The mind of Christ allows us to see from his perspective. In the natural realm, our eyes send an invisible signal to our brain and our brain tells us what we are seeing. The brain is the translator, so it is in the Spirit. The mind of Christ is what gives us spiritual sight. People who don't have the mind of Christ are spiritually blind and ignorant.

"In whom the god of this world hath blinded the minds of them which believe not, lest the light of the glorious gospel of Christ, who is the image of God, should shine unto them." (2 Corinthians 4:4)

When the gospel is received, spiritual sight is received. Wherever there is unbelief there is spiritual blindness and ignorance. Unbelief is also spelled d-e-c-e-p-t-i-o-n.

There are three predominant worldviews today. *The secular worldview, the theological worldview and a Biblical Kingdom worldview* that believing believers have as they see the world through the mind of Christ. Sadly to say most professing

Christians have a secular worldview, which is why many people who have eternal life vote for men and woman who are not pro-life. They don't understand reality from God's perspective and so for less important reasons they vote for someone who stands in direct opposition to the Kingdom of God. The secular worldview is the worldview of much of the young generation. Whatever makes you feel good; whatever makes you happy, whatever floats your boat. These are all phrases that are rooted in secularism. The secular worldview is like the Greeks' worldview in the New Testament who were seeking wisdom and philosophy. The universities and the media push this worldview at us twenty-four hours a day seven days a week. Sensual, sexual and anything goes in the secular worldview. The main focus of this worldview is "self" and "feelings".

The theological worldview is the worldview that the Pharisees had in the New Testament. They saw the world through their understanding of God and his word. They didn't see the world through the word; they saw the word through the world. Meaning they didn't see from God's perspective. So the religious people of the day knew the book of the Law but when the Author, finisher and fulfiller was standing before them they couldn't see him. This worldview separates itself from the people it's supposed to reach. The theological worldview is a worldview that has a *form of godliness but denies the power thereof.* This is the worldview that does violence to Jesus and the body of Christ. This is the worldview of Islam or even communism. Communism makes the government God. Muslims kill people because of their false perspective of God. This is a dangerous worldview that seeks to rule by power and force based on a bad theology or a bad and incorrect view of God. This blindness leads to darkness and many innocent people die because of some people's false perspective of God. The twin towers were knocked down on 9/11/01 because of a false theological worldview called Islam. This is a very harmful worldview. It's also the worldview that screamed, "crucify him" to Jesus. The Jewish people cheered as Jesus rode into Jerusalem on a donkey proclaiming himself to be the Messiah. They thought he was going to free them politically from Rome. However, in that time he actually came to free them spiritually from themselves and the devil. Their cheers turned into screams as soon as Jesus didn't do what their bad theology or eschatology wanted him to do. They thought Isaiah 63 was going to happen before Isaiah 53 and they were sadly mistaken. Bad theology causes people to turn on God when he doesn't do what they think he should do. Unfortunately, this view is also in churches now. This worldview causes Christians to blame God for things that the enemy does. The definition of blaming God for something he hasn't done is just plain - deception.

Kingdom worldview is an integrated worldview. When Jesus taught his disciples how to pray in Matthew 6, he said, *"on earth as it is in heaven."* He integrates heaven and earth and calls it God's will. A lot of the church is waiting to go to heaven when Jesus wants heaven to come to earth. The secular worldview through human wisdom tries to rule the earth by intellect. The theological or false theological worldview seeks to dominate by power, force or any means necessary. The kingdom worldview dominates through prayer and obedience to God. As citizens of the Kingdom our obedience to Jesus brings his leadership to circumstances, people and problems. We do this through gentleness, meekness, compassion and love. It takes faith to see the world and people from Jesus' perspective. The Father is consummating all things under Jesus' headship, lordship or leadership. It always takes faith to believe this because the news and even the circumstances in our lives, families, churches and finances seem to show different results. It takes faith to believe what we do not fully see. We as believers who are seated in heavenly places in Christ Jesus must see from the perspective that Jesus is Lord even though all things don't appear to be submitted to him just yet. Circumstances don't define who Jesus is; Jesus was defined by the Father's voice alone.

Jesus must define us; his perspective of reality must be ours or we are either ignorant or deceived. We must see others and ourselves through his eyes. *The mind of Christ is the only mind necessary in the Kingdom of God.* We have been given his mind so we can be of one mind and be unified about his will and not our own. The mind of Christ proves the will of God because it clearly sees the will of God. The kingdom worldview is simply seeing the world from the King's perspective. Our perception really matters. If we misperceive reality, we are deceived. The Kingdom worldview that Jesus displayed puts our focus on the present moment. Our worldview affects how we use our time and resources. *The integrated worldview that links heaven and earth together has an eternal perspective that focuses on the present moment.* The will of God is in the present moment. When Jesus began his ministry, he started with these words, *"Repent, the Kingdom of God is at hand."* (See Matthew 4:17.) This is Jesus telling people to change the way they think God's power and resources are available now because I am here. Here Jesus is putting the focus on the present moment and introducing a new way of seeing reality. Jesus was saying all the prophecies are standing before you right now; the word was made flesh and is dwelling among you. God's power is present to heal; his salvation is for the now. Today is the day of salvation. The kingdom worldview believes all things are coming under Jesus' leadership. That is why we call him Lord. This worldview that links heaven and earth gives us a perspective that values the present more than the past or the future. A religious theological worldview always looks to the past to define the future. We as people of the kingdom have to learn that God has tomorrow all figured out and just obey and enjoy him today.

Secular humanism is just simply a lack of Biblical truth. The religious theological worldview is a worldview that comes from human perspective. It lacks faith in God but knows things about God. The kingdom worldview is a worldview of faith that believes the word of God and practices obedience to the scriptures by being led by the Holy Spirit. There is no unbelief in the kingdom, which means through faith we accomplish that which God has ordained for us to do.

"Who through faith subdued kingdom, wrought righteousness, obtained promises, stopped the mouth of lions." (Hebrews 11:33)

Here we see that faith causes to "do" not just believe. Faith is an essential ingredient for entering into the Kingdom and living a life that is pleasing to Christ our King. Sometimes it's hard to think and believe the message of the kingdom when our society is screaming rebellion against God in every way possible. The culture we live in is so against God as creator scientists are trying to clone people. People are literally trying to create life on their own. Secular culture is so against God that it will pay to kill children in the name of pro-choice or women's rights. God gives life and man is taking it away because of the love of money. The society we live in is at war with everything that God is and everything his kingdom stands for.

> *"Thou hast put all things in subjection under his feet. For in that he put all in subjection under him, he left nothing that is not put under him. But now we see not yet all things put under him. But we see Jesus, who was made a little lower than the angels for the suffering of death, crowned with glory and honor; that he by the grace of God should taste death for every man."* (Hebrews 2:8-9)

In reality all things are under Jesus; however, in the visible world we can't see it fully just yet. That is why the writer of Hebrews is telling us who we see and that he tasted death for everyman. Meaning our focus and the focus of everyman should be upon Jesus and what he has done. Here we are focusing on Jesus who tasted death for every man, rather than everything that doesn't outwardly appear to be under his feet. The most amazing thing about the kingdom worldview is that we are to keep our eyes on King Jesus. If we are going to maintain a kingdom worldview, we must look unto Jesus continually.

There is a difference between the King and his kingdom. Hebrews 13:8 says, *"Jesus Christ the same yesterday, and today, and forever."* Here we learn something very interesting. Jesus never changes; he remains the same. He has no need to change. Nothing he has ever said or done could ever be improved upon. He is so good there is no room for him to be made better. He changes not; this is incomprehensible to the carnal mind. Only the mind of Christ can see this mystery of Christ's complete supremacy. Jesus has no need for change in any way. However, the Kingdom of God is continually increasing, hence *"of the increase of his government and peace there shall be no end."* (Isaiah 9:6 a) Jesus is the beginning and the ending; there is no beginning but him and there is no end but him. His kingdom is continually increasing, and he himself is never changing. The only logical explanation is simply because he said so. To maintain a kingdom worldview, we need a new operating system called the mind of Christ. With this new operating system we need a whole new value system. The value system and the operating system work together like the hardware and the software of a computer. Both have been provided for us in the scriptures and paid for by the blood of Jesus and are manifested through the Holy Spirit.

"If ye then be risen with Christ, seek those things which are above, where Christ sitteth on the right hand of God. Set your affection on things above, not on things on the earth." (Colossians 3:1-2)

Our affections must be set on Jesus and what he is doing. We are risen with Christ so that we can be seated with Christ in heavenly places.

Ephesians 2:6 states, *"And hath raised us up together, and made us sit together in heavenly places in Christ Jesus."* Someone who is seated with Christ is obviously someone who has a kingdom worldview. Jesus paid for us with a crown of thorns so that we may have the mind of Christ. He descended so we could ascend and be seated with him. This is a place of privilege and favor that was paid for by Jesus. Therefore, we must honor his sacrifice by living from his perspective. How we see the world will greatly affect how we treat the world.

"And Jesus went forth, and saw a great multitude, and was moved with compassion toward them, and he healed their sick." (Matthew 14:14)

Adam LiVecchi

What Jesus saw directly affected what he did. Remember perception means everything. Compassion leads the King to action and so if we are going to follow him we need his perspective. His perspective is what empowers us to take action. The same compassion that moved him must move us if we are really following him. Our king is full of passion and compassion. When we are full of him we do what he did. The Kingdom is continually moving forward and change is inevitable if we are going to follow Jesus. Jesus doesn't just want to change the world he wants to create a new heaven. Kingdom people understand change without compromising God's word or ways. Jesus' lordship will increase in your life and as it does people will come to see and know who Jesus really is through you.

CHAPTER 3

DEFINING OR RE-DEFINING THE KINGDOM

We will briefly start this chapter by stating what the Kingdom of God is not. The kingdom of God is not the false religion of Jehovah witnesses. Their gathering places are called "kingdom hall." The church is not the Kingdom. The church can go into apostasy through hypocrisy and false doctrine while the kingdom can only increase. The church is who we are; the kingdom is where we live. The church has membership and the kingdom has citizenship. In church, order can be broken, but in the kingdom of God order was broken once and satan was cast down and order has been perfect ever since. The gates of hell cannot prevail against the church, while hell can't even come close to the kingdom of God because it's in another world. Often churches need revival because they are dead. *However, the kingdom never needs a revival because nothing is dead in the kingdom.* When we see the big shot TV preacher begging for people to give him money to buy a building, the building is not the kingdom. The bank account where the money is kept is not the kingdom either. I am not against money or TV ministry or even asking people to sow into a vision that God has entrusted to a man. I am simply saying we should never call something the kingdom when it isn't— that would be called deception. Acts 17:24 states, *"God that made the world and all things therein, seeing that he is Lord of heaven and earth, dwelleth not in temples made with hands."* The kingdom may come to the building, but the building is not the kingdom.

The kingdom of God does not shake. Haggai 2:7-8 says, *"And I will shake all nations, and the desire of all nations shall come: and I will fill this house with glory, saith the LORD of hosts. The silver is mine, and the gold is mine, saith the LORD of hosts."* When God begins to shake the nations as he has promised, church buildings will shake and break but his kingdom people will arise and shine. The true church lives in the kingdom. The message of the kingdom has been distorted to be about everything other than Jesus' supreme leadership. The false religion of the Jehovah witnesses has falsely represented the kingdom of God. A lot of orthodox Christianity has misrepresented the message of the kingdom through covetousness and materialism. Also insecure fear based leaders have used the message of *"kingdom order"* to control people for quite some time. There are many other things that people call kingdom that are not, but if I took time to comment on each of them this would turn into another book. These sober realities are very unfortunate; therefore, we must define and redefine from a biblical perspective what the Kingdom of God really is. *Any authoritative perspective on the kingdom of God must be rooted in the scriptures.* Extra-biblical experiences are good, but they are not authoritative. If any of these experiences are anti-biblical they are to be rejected and corrected both personally and corporately.

Sadly to say most charismatic leaders don't have the courage to refute many people's bogus claims, but there are people who really will let Jesus be the Lord of their life. However, there are voices emerging that will not be silent in the generation to come concerning error. Remember there is no error in the kingdom of God. Therefore as citizens of the Kingdom we can't be afraid of speaking the truth. *"For there must be also heresies among you, that they which are approved may be made manifest among you."* (1 Corinthians 11:19) Those who are approved for the work of God stand up and speak the word of God where it is being, watered

The Increase of His Government

down, compromised, misused for personal gain or just plain taught incorrectly. The Kingdom is a culture where confrontation is normal. One of the ways the Kingdom advances is through confrontation of light and darkness and truth and error.

"Jesus answered and said unto them, Ye do err, not knowing the scriptures, nor the power of God." (Matthew 22:29)

The bible is not the kingdom of God, but it paints the only clear picture of the Kingdom that is reliable. When the kingdom comes to the church, it comes to purge it and reinstate Jesus' Lordship by the word of the Lord. In Revelation 2 -3, the church was out of alignment with the Kingdom of God. So Jesus spoke to line the church back up with the Kingdom. In the kingdom of God, there is no dysfunction, because everyone always obeys the King. The abiding place is for the obedient. When we disobey, it's like we take a step out of the kingdom for a moment. An example in the natural would be a teenager who smokes. If he is not allowed to smoke in the home, he will step outside because disobedience inside the home is not an option. The Kingdom is where Jesus is ruling and reigning, which means there is no sin. The King died to free us from sin and death. There is nothing dead in the Kingdom because King Jesus died so we can enter into him and have eternal life. The most beautiful picture of the Kingdom of God is Christ Jesus because he always did what was pleasing to the Father. He was sinless; he lived the model Christian life because he was Christ. Anything that is truly about or for the Kingdom of God will make us more Christ like. If it isn't seen in Jesus, it's probably not the Kingdom. If it doesn't make Jesus seen, heard and known it's not Kingdom. The message of the Kingdom is a revelation of the King. All of Jesus' words, actions, signs, and wonders were in complete subjection to the Father; that my friend is Kingdom.

Romans 14:17 says, *"For the Kingdom of God is not meat and drink; but righteousness, and peace, and joy in the Holy Ghost."* Paul said this by divine inspiration because people were making a huge deal out of the food people ate. Some of the Roman Christians were offended by people eating meat. However, there are several things we can learn from this. *The kingdom of God does not abide or dwell in the natural but it invades the natural realm.* Here Paul the Apostle defines what the Kingdom is and is not. He also does this again in a different manner in his epistle to the Corinthians.

"For the Kingdom of God is not in word, but in power." (1 Corinthians 4:20)

The Kingdom doesn't just come in word; it comes in power also. It should be the authentic word that releases power, or the authentic power defined by the word. The gospel of the Kingdom is displayed two ways: proclamation and demonstration or demonstration and explanation. We will touch on this point in a more focused way later in the book. A principle that can be extracted from both of these verses is that "the kingdom of God is not natural;, it's supernatural." Remember what is supernatural to us is natural to God. He is naturally supernatural, and he is making us just like him in Jesus.

As we define righteousness, peace and joy in the Holy Spirit, we will see Jesus. Jeremiah 23:5-6 says, *"Behold, the days come, saith the LORD, that I will raise unto David a righteous Branch, and a King shall reign and prosper, and shall execute judgment and justice in the earth. In his days Judah shall be saved, and Israel shall dwell safely: and this is his name whereby he shall be called, THE LORD OUR RIGHTEOUSNESS."* Righteousness is a person, and he is the second and better covenant. The concept and benefits of covenant are crucial in the Kingdom of God. Everything in the Kingdom is from the place of covenant and relationship. Previously we learned that Jesus gave himself for us in doing so he purchased us the Kingdom of God. That is really good news. He is the merchant who sold everything and bought the pearl of great price.

"Again, the kingdom of heaven is like unto a merchant man, seeking goodly pearls: Who, when he had found one pearl of great price, went and sold all that he had, and bought it." (Matthew 13:45-46)

Remember Jesus came to seek and to save that which was lost. It was him who pursued us. Often times we make things about us that are not really about us.

He purchased us for himself. Ephesians 2:13-14 states, *"But now in Christ Jesus ye who sometimes were far off are made nigh by the blood of Christ. For he is our peace, who hath made both one, and hath broken down the middle wall of partition between us."* Here we see that peace is a person his name is Christ Jesus. The cross slays cultural enmity, which means there is no prejudice in the Kingdom of God. Jesus our righteousness died in our place and made peace with God on our behalf. He stood in the gap and bore the wrath we deserve; he is our righteousness and our peace. His blood speaks righteousness over us and his cross slays culturally enmity and makes us to be at peace with God and one another. He died to live in us, not just so that we can go to heaven when we die. We were created to dwell in his presence. Righteousness and peace are not enough. It was for the joy that was set before Jesus that he endured the cross. Joy endures, the atmosphere of the King and his Kingdom is joy. Peace is amazing but joy is like peace on steroids. Peace sleeps in storms, but joy endures the cross. Peace is more powerful than a storm, but joy is more powerful than death.

Psalm 16:11 states, *"Thou wilt show me the path of life: in thy presence is fullness of joy; at thy right hand there are pleasures for evermore."* In God's presence is the fullness of joy and pleasures forevermore. This verse is amazing; it truly teaches us about the king and his kingdom. There is fullness of joy in his presence, meaning everything in the Kingdom is abundantly overflowing. The duration of these pleasures are eternal. God is abundantly eternal. The Kingdom is righteousness, peace and joy in the Holy Spirit. Joy is a really big deal; joy is a fruit of the Spirit. Joy is clearly found in God's presence.

"These things have I spoken unto you, that my joy might remain in you, and that your joy might be full." (John 15:11)

Hearing the Lord's voice is how joy is released to us. Jesus continually lived full of the Holy Spirit, which means we need to live full. When we are truly filed with the Spirit, we naturally overflow. When men see our good works, our Father in heaven is glorified. That's what it looks like to be hidden in Christ. We obey Jesus and they don't see us but rather they see the Father as we obey his Son. We were created for his good pleasure, and at his right hand there are pleasures for us forever as we live in his presence. The Kingdom life is about us being with him where he is and him coming to invade where we live. His invasion comes through our obedience.

Before we define the Kingdom more let us see what we learned about the Kingdom in the life of Christ. Jesus is the Lord our righteousness. He is the righteous one because he never sinned; we become righteousness because he died to forgive our sins. Jesus became sin and we became the righteousness of God in him. Jesus was dealing with a sick sinner and he put righteousness on the sinner by forgiving and healing him.

> "*Whether is it easier to say to the sick of the palsy, Thy sins be forgiven thee; or to say, Arise, and take up thy bed, and walk? But that ye may know that the Son of man hath power on earth to forgive sins, (he saith to the sick of the palsy,) I say unto thee, Arise, and take up thy bed, and go thy way into thine house. And immediately he arose, took up the bed, and went forth before them all; insomuch that they were all amazed, and glorified God, saying, We never saw it on this fashion.*" (Mark 2:9-12)

Here Jesus used healing as an illustration of forgiveness. Sickness to your body is like sin to your soul. It was Jesus' authority that released healing, which illustrated forgiveness and brought the man who was sick of palsy into full restoration. Another time the Pharisees were going to stone a woman caught in adultery. It just so happens that the man wasn't brought with her to be stoned as well. Anyway Jesus said whoever is sinless throw the first stone. All the religious devils left. The word he spoke put righteousness on her. He forgave her and freed her from death. His righteousness was imputed to her as he spoke and she believed. You know Jesus is speaking when the religious people start leaving. Sorry I had to get that one in there.

Let's see peace in the life and ministry of Jesus. Mark 4:37-39 states,

> *"And there arose a great storm of wind, and the waves beat into the ship, so that it was now full. And he was in the hinder part of the ship, asleep on a pillow: and they awake him, and say unto him, Master, carest thou not that we perish? And he arose, and rebuked the wind, and said unto the sea, Peace, be still. And the wind ceased, and there was a great calm."*

Jesus had peace, which means he could sleep in a storm. We have authority over the storms we can sleep in. Jesus had peace; therefore, he could release it simply because he had it. The Kingdom of God is righteousness, peace and joy in the Holy Spirit. So when he released the Kingdom on the storm, the storm had to be still in the presence of the Kingdom. The Kingdom was released by the words of the King. The Kingdom is manifested by the declaration of the word of God. In our life, Jesus will manifest himself as we obey him. As we obey his word, the Kingdom comes. We have access to the Kingdom by faith in the King's word. The Kingdom of God is not like a credit card. In the Kingdom you can only give what you have.

"And they feared exceedingly, and said one to another, What manner of man is this, that even the wind and the sea obey him?" (Mark 4:41)

This was a sign that truly made them wonder. When the Kingdom comes, it will always point to the King. Anything that has the label kingdom on it must point to the Jesus of the scriptures. Jesus was in a real storm, and he had peace. He gave us his peace because he knows that this life has many storms in it. Peace in our life can calm the storms in other people's lives as we obey Jesus and speak what we hear him saying. Peace calms storms and joy endures the cross.

Nehemiah 8:10 states *"The joy of the Lord is our strength"*. Biblically we know that to be true, but often we lack the experience of it in our daily lives. In the Kingdom of God our doctrine and our experience must be married to manifest God's will. Righteousness and peace consummate in joy. Righteousness plus peace equals joy. Joy divided by two is righteousness and peace. Love's greatest exploit was empowered by joy and carried out by humility for love's sake.

"Looking unto Jesus the author and finisher of our faith; who for the joy that was set before him endured the cross, despising the shame, and is set down at the right hand of the throne of God." (Hebrews 12:2)

Speaking peace to a storm is amazing, but being chastised so others could have peace is even more amazing. Enduring the suffering of the cross was accomplished through joy. Joy is what empowered Jesus' statement *"It is finished."* Jesus who is the author and finisher of our faith cried, "It is finished" from Calvary. This was accomplished through his humility to submit to the will of the Father. The joy the Father gave him was enough to endure the cross.

"And being found in fashion as a man, he humbled himself, and became obedient unto death, even the death of the cross." (Philippians 2:8)

Humility causes us to obey God. A humble person is not someone who is quiet and doesn't say or do anything. A humble person is someone who does what God says. Jesus is our role model; we are to be like him because that is the whole point of the Christian life. As we define the Kingdom, we must see clearly that Jesus paid for it with his merit so that we can enter into it. His blood speaks a better word. He was raised from the dead so that we could be born again. He left his throne so we could ascend with him and be seated in heavenly places with and in him.

We clearly understand that the Kingdom of God is righteousness, peace and joy in the Holy Spirit. Jesus became sin so we could be made the righteousness of God him, see 2 Corinthians 5:21.

"But he was wounded for our transgressions, he was bruised for our iniquities: the chastisement of our peace was upon him; and with his stripes we are healed." (Isaiah 53:5)

Christ our King was chastised and tortured for our peace. We must value the Kingdom as much as Jesus' life. He paid it all for us; his pearl of great price was his very own life. We must learn to remember and value what he has done. When we learn to remember, our hearts stay tender. A hard heart and joy are just not in the same equation. Jesus' greatest accomplishment was through joy. Joy is not merely laughter, although it very well may be a piece of it. Joy is what allows and empowers one to endure their darkest hour and come out victorious. Jesus was a man of sorrows, but his joy empowered him to endure the cross. In this life we will have sorrows, persecutions, tribulations and hard times, but his joy will get us through. It's through the empowering presence of joy that the Apostle Paul tells us to *"rejoice always,"* 1 Thessalonians 5:16. He wrote this from a prison cell not a penthouse mansion. Our circumstances cannot define us; the Kingdom must empower us to reveal Jesus through our lives as we yield to him and let his atmosphere be ours. Jesus' atmosphere must shape our circumstances. What he says about us is what really matters. People of the Kingdom don't live in their circumstances they live at their circumstances.

If we read the Bible and just compare what Jesus said to what other people said we would clearly see that what he said is incomparably greater than any other person in scriptures. Jesus said to Philip, *"If you have seen me you have seen the Father."* See John 14:9. The writer of Hebrews explains this statement in a profound way.

> *"Who being the brightness of his glory, and the express image of his person, and upholding all things by the word of his power, when he had by himself purged our sins, sat down on the right hand of the Majesty on high."* (Hebrews 1:3)

Jesus is the light that emanates from the Father's very being. The Father overflows Jesus. When the Father speaks, Jesus comes forth. He is the Father in the visible world. The light that shines off Jesus' face is everything the Father is. The depth of the triune God reality is the most fascinating thing about Biblical Christianity.

The most profound thing in and about the Kingdom is God himself. As Jesus was teaching his disciples to pray, he defined the Kingdom in a profoundly simple manner. I mentioned earlier that if you have seen Jesus you have seen the Father, for the reason of clarifying Jesus' definition before I give it. I am laying out a context to Jesus' definition of the Kingdom.

"And lead us not into temptation, but deliver us from evil: For thine is the kingdom, and the power, and the glory, forever. Amen." (Matthew 6:13)

Jesus is clearly praying to the Father. This prayer is often referred to as either the "Our Father" or the "Lord's Prayer." You can call it whatever you want. In reality, it's Jesus praying to the Father. It's not really about what we call it but it's more about praying it and allowing our life to be the answer to our own prayers as Jesus conforms us to his image. When Jesus said, "thine is the Kingdom" he is referring to the Father. Jesus defines the Kingdom as the Father. Later on in the Gospel of John before he is crucified he said, "If you have seen me you have seen the Father." Jesus is the clearest picture of the Father. He is the exact image of what Father looks like, acts like and speaks like. Jesus only did what he saw the Father do; he only said what he heard the Father say. Jesus shows us the Father and perfectly models the Kingdom life. Jesus didn't push the Kingdom into the future; he brought it into the present. He pulled it into the now. If we want to follow him, we must understand that the timing of God's Kingdom is now! We can't push the Kingdom into the future and really follow Jesus now! He shows us what God is like and what man can live like when we are wholly yielded to God like he was. It pleased the Father to bruise him, according to Isaiah 53:10. Jesus laid down his will at the expense of his own life. That is what loyalty looks like in the Kingdom. Loyalty is the behavior of royalty.

As we continue to let Jesus and the scriptures re-define and define the Kingdom, we will get a fresh revelation of who Jesus is, who we are, and what he has for us. The Greek word for Kingdom has four meanings. They are simple and yet profound. No one interprets the scriptures like scripture. The scriptures are God's opinion, and that is the opinion that really matters. So the Greek word for Kingdom is "basilia." It means royalty, rule, reign, and realm. Each one of those words has very simple but clear meanings. **Royalty** speaks of Jesus as our king and what his blood has made us. All of the citizens of the Kingdom are royalty and have an inheritance.

> *"And from Jesus Christ, who is the faithful witness, and the first begotten of the dead, and the prince of the kings of the earth. Unto him that loved us, and washed us from our sins in his own blood, And hath made us kings and priests unto God and his Father; to him be glory and dominion forever and ever. Amen."* (Revelation 1:5-6)

Here we learn that the blood of Jesus has washed us from our sins and made us Kings and Priests. The blood of Jesus doesn't just save us from hell. It creates us for Kingdom purpose clothes us with identity and authority as Christ's very own purchased possessions. Royalty speaks of the King and everyone in his kingdom. Not everyone in every kingdom is royalty. As a matter of fact, the Kingdom of God is the only kingdom where everyone in the Kingdom is royalty, simply because of who the King is. The most amazing thing about the Kingdom is the King. Often this is not true of earthly kingdoms. The three other meanings of the word

"Kingdom" in Greek are rule, reign and realm. The greatness of who Jesus is will become even more apparent after we define these three words in the context of defining his Kingdom. **Rule** refers to the people he is ruling over. Here are two brief examples:

"Beside the chief of Solomon's officers which were over the work, three thousand and three hundred, which ruled over the people that wrought in the work." (Kings 5:16)

"And he gave them into the hand of the heathen; and they that hated them ruled over them." (Psalm 106:41)

A TV preacher or even an author doesn't have the right to define the Kingdom. Only Jesus does through the scriptures. Here the Bible is defining God's kingdom. Our traditional beliefs may be ok, but not if they are not clearly in agreement with scripture. Jesus rules over all of humanity, which is why he will judge all of humanity. **Reign** would be the time frame of the King's rule and realm. Here is a brief example where the word reign speaks of the duration of time the King is ruling for.

"David was thirty years old when he began to reign, and he reigned forty years." (2 Samuel 5:4)

Here are several more examples of the word reigned being used to describe the duration of a King's kingdom, 1 Samuel 13:1, and 2 Samuel 2:10. **Realm** would be the geographical area where the King is ruling. Here are a few examples of the word realm being used to describe the geography of a Kingdom.

"In the first year of Darius the son of Ahasuerus, of the seed of the Medes, which was made king over the realm of the Chaldeans." (Daniel 9:1)

"And now will I show thee the truth. Behold, there shall stand up yet three kings in Persia; and the fourth shall be far richer than they all: and by his strength through his riches he shall stir up all against the realm of Grecia." (Daniel 11:2)

God's Kingdom is from everlasting to everlasting; therefore, his reign is forever because he is eternal. Jesus is the Alpha and Omega, the beginning and the ending; therefore, his Kingdom is from everlasting to everlasting. Something interesting about the Bible is that time is measured by delegated authority. Here are some scriptures to illustrate this reality: Luke 1:5, Matthew 2:1, Isaiah 6:1, Ruth 1:1, and 1 Kings 2:1. There are many more but that was just a brief illustration of the concept of time being measured by delegated authority. The concept of delegated authority measuring time is awesome because it points directly to Christ Jesus.

"And Jesus came and spoke unto them, saying, All power is given unto me in heaven and in earth." (Matthew 28:18)

The word power here in Greek is "exosia." It literally means authority. All authority has been given to him. The authority from heaven towards earth was given to him, see Revelation 1:18. So again we see that his realm is heaven and earth. Also we learn that all the authority has been given to Jesus. This is so true that his life and death splits time itself in half. Even atheist scientists know this is the year 2012 A.D. 2012 years after the death of Jesus Christ. If he was only a man, his death couldn't split time itself in half. All authority has been given to him, so his life and death literally splits time itself in half. The scripture declares that he is Lord of heaven and earth and time itself testifies to this truth.

"At that time Jesus answered and said, I thank thee, O Father, Lord of heaven and earth, because thou hast hid these things from the wise and prudent, and hast revealed them unto babes." (Matthew 11:25)

So we clearly see from the last two scriptures that Jesus' realm is heaven and earth. This is absolute truth yet it's not always visible in the circumstances on earth. Everything on the earth including you and I don't necessarily seem to be under the full influence of Jesus. In spite of what things look like Jesus is the Lord of heaven and earth. The authority was the Father's and he gave it to Jesus and Jesus gave it to us. His authority is our inheritance because we belong to him. When we obey his commands and come under his authority we then have access to his power for his glory.

Kingdom life is about obeying what the King says so that his purposes are established as his Kingdom advances. *Obedience to what Jesus commanded would be an accurate definition of Christianity.* Most of what we call Christianity God calls hypocrisy or even apostasy. Our assignment is to teach people to obey all things that Jesus commanded, which is not possible for one hour on a Sunday. It takes a lifestyle of devotion to Jesus and commitment to one another.

"Teaching them to observe all things whatsoever I have commanded you: and, lo, I am with you always even unto the end of the world. Amen." (Matthew 28:20)

We can't do this if we don't know all things that he commanded. If we don't do all that he commanded how can we teach others to? Therefore, the Kingdom work starts within. We learn what he said to do, and we learn to obey. Then we teach others and invite them into the Kingdom of God. In the Kingdom, everything is under the wise leadership of the King. Our job is to bring people to Jesus and to teach them the benefits of his leadership. Wherever there are problems or lack, it's because someone or a group of people are rejecting Jesus' leadership. If someone persecutes a believer for his or her righteousness, it's because the unbeliever is under the wrong leadership. The Kingdom of God does not shake because the King does not change. Jesus Christ is the same yesterday, today and forever. Jesus' rule or dominion is everyone. His reign is forever, and his realm is heaven and earth and even in us. If we search ourselves and our churches and society, we will discover that full obedience to Jesus is very hard to come by let alone sustain. Everything is under Jesus feet in truth according to the scriptures but experientially most of the world and church are actually in rebellion to him and what he commanded. We must allow the Holy Spirit to search us and teach us to submit ourselves to his leadership. Before we focus on everything and everyone and all kinds of injustices that are not practically under Jesus' feet, we need to come under his wise leadership ourselves. Beginning from the inside out. Religion works from the outside in, while relationship with Jesus begins and works from the inside out.

> *"Thou hast put all things in subjection under his feet. For in that he put all in subjection under him, he left nothing that is not put under him.* ***But now we see not yet all things put under him.*** *But we see Jesus, who was made a little lower than the angels for the suffering of death, crowned with glory and honor; that he by the grace of God should taste death for every man."* (Hebrews 2:8-9)

I am commenting on the bold phrase above. Even the writer of Hebrews knew that we do not see all things put under Jesus' feet. All things don't clearly appear to be under his leadership. Here we learn to focus on Jesus and not what is not happening We must focus on what Jesus has done and is doing if we want to be a part of what he will do. Jesus is the center and the focus of Kingdom life. As we look to him and obey him, other people come into his Kingdom and come under his authority. The commands of the Kingdom are to make us like the King, which helps bring people to him as we are his reflection in the earth. This is our mission if we choose to accept it.

CHAPTER 4
THE SUPREMACY OF JESUS CHRIST

Every Kingdom must have a King. Without a King it's not really a Kingdom. What the king is like greatly defines the Kingdom, especially because Kingdoms are not democracies. In democracies there are checks and balances. In Kingdoms there is a king, and he is Sovereign, meaning what he says goes. The central doctrine of the Kingdom of God is that Jesus Christ is Lord. The Kingdom of God has a King; he is the King of kings and above him there is no other. Before we go into the economy or the currency or the laws of the Kingdom, first we must know the King. Jesus is not like any other King in all of history. He is fully God and fully man. He is God's only begotten Son who spoke the world into existence. He is the creator, redeemer, sustainer and judge. He manifested in the flesh and was also born of a virgin.

"For unto us a child is born, unto us a Son is given: and the government shall be upon his shoulder: and his name shall be called Wonderful, Counselor, The mighty God, The everlasting Father, The prince of peace." (Isaiah 9:6)

Jesus has many names; he has been given the name above all names. He is crowned with many crowns simply because he is the King of Kings. He has so much authority; he is the only King who has a kingdom of kings.

The more intimately acquainted we are with Jesus; the more his supremacy will be seen in our life. It's our intimacy with him that releases his supremacy to and through us. When we obey his word and have access to his power, our lives bring him glory. Jesus modeled this with his Father. Nothing and no circumstances that Jesus entered into were bigger than his Father. The supremacy of Christ is seen all through the scriptures. If you search the scriptures deeply, you will clearly find the supremacy of Christ all through the Bible. You will see his victorious triumph over death itself. Jesus led captivity captive; he not only had victory over death, but over life and all of the circumstances that life on this planet could throw at him, including the devil himself.

"Wherefore God also hath highly exalted him, and given him a name which is above every name." (Philippians 2:9)

Jesus has been given a name above all names, which means he has the final say. All authority has been given to him; therefore, he is supreme. Above him there is no other. There is no court or government higher than him. He is the high and lofty who inhabits all of eternity, yet he can fit on the inside of us.

"For thus saith the high and lofty One that inhabiteth eternity, whose name is Holy; I dwell in the high and holy place, with him also that is of a contrite and humble spirit, to revive the spirit of the humble, and to revive the heart of the contrite ones." (Isaiah 57:15)

He overflows from eternity into the very hearts of men. He is the high and lofty one who inhabits eternity, yet he humbled himself to the death of a cross for you and me. Truly there is no one like him. In most kingdoms, people give their life for the king, but in the Kingdom of God King Jesus gave himself for us. In governments that have *"supposedly free"* health care the people pay for it by high taxes, but in the Kingdom of God Jesus paid for our health care by the stripes on his back. Jesus gives joy unspeakable his riches are unsearchable. He is so much more than enough; he is the most generous person I know. The supremacy of Christ is not just about Jesus ruling everything around us but also ruling everything in us. The last sentence clearly defines true kingdom purpose, which is to make us Christ like. In the Kingdom of God, Christ is formed in us and we rule and reign with him as we simply obey what he says. The Father is glorified as we are led by the Holy Spirit to obey and follow Jesus. The Kingdom life is not just about what we believe or profess, but it's also about us being in complete submission to Jesus and his teachings. Jesus gave us the comforter because without him we couldn't obey Jesus. Jesus also knew that if we would obey him we would need the comforter because following Jesus can put us in some uncomfortable situations.

Christ's supremacy is about making the impossible the possible. *In the Kingdom of God, the impossible is logical because we have been given the mind of Christ.* The mind of Christ was a free gift to us but Jesus paid for it with a crown of thorns. The Kingdom life is not only about going to heaven, but it's about heaven invading earth as Christ is formed. He is formed in us as he speaks to us. God moves through us as we obey him. Even before Jesus manifested in the flesh his supremacy was clearly seen, even by the heathen. In the book of Daniel, God manifests his faithfulness to faithful men.

"With the merciful thou wilt show thyself merciful; with an upright man thou wilt show thyself upright; With the pure thou wilt show thyself pure; and with the froward thou wilt show thyself froward." (Psalm 18:25-26)

The book of Daniel shows a great picture of this scripture. Through uncompromised devotion to the word of God, the Kingdom is manifested. This is eternally true because even before the writer of Hebrews wrote, *"Jesus Christ is the same yesterday today and forever,"* he was. So in the book of Daniel, Jerusalem was taken captive according to Jeremiah's Prophecy, see Jeremiah 36 and Daniel 1:1.

They were taken captive because they had no regard for the word of the Lord. This captivity meant a great slaughter of the Jewish people; they also became free slave labor to Babylon for seventy years. In the midst of the exile, there was a faithful remnant from the tribe of Judah who would not compromise.

A law is made in Babylon stating that everyone must worship an image of Nebuchadnezzar. In the book of Exodus, God gave a command that he alone is to be worshipped. Anytime people friends, family or even civil government is in opposition to the Scriptures our allegiance must be to Jesus first.

> *"Thou shalt have no other gods before me. Thou shalt not make unto thee any graven image, or any likeness of any thing that is in heaven above, or that is in the earth beneath, or that is in the water under the earth: Thou shalt not bow down thyself to them, nor serve them: for I the LORD thy God am a jealous God, visiting the iniquity of the fathers upon the children unto the third and fourth generation of them that hate me; And showing mercy unto thousands of them that love me, and keep my commandments."* (Exodus 20:3-6)

However, Shadrach, Meshach and Abednego refused to bow their knees to anyone but the God of heaven. This act of courageous love and obedience to God caused Jesus to manifest himself on their behalf. John 14:21 says, "He that hath my commandments, and keepeth them, he it is that loveth me: and he that loveth me shall be loved of my Father, and I will love him, and will manifest myself to him." It's so amazing to see this verse or truth in manifestation even before Jesus said it.

> Daniel 3:23-25 states, *"And these three men, Shadrach, Meshach, and Abed–nego, fell down bound into the midst of the burning fiery furnace. Then Nebuchadnezzar the king was astonished, and rose up in haste, and spoke, and said unto his counselors, Did not we cast three men bound into the midst of the*

> *fire? They answered and said unto the king, True, O king. He answered and said, Lo, I see four men loose, walking in the midst of the fire, and they have no hurt; and the form of the fourth is like the Son of God."*

It's very interesting how a heathen King can immediately recognize who Jesus is. This is a masterpiece painting of Christ's supremacy. Jesus is the only one who can save men from the fires of hell. He is the only name under heaven in which men might be saved from the fires of hell. Jesus isn't just the name above all names, but he is the only name under heaven in which men might be saved. When Jesus shows up the impossible becomes possible. We know this is Jesus in the fire because the scripture says so, and another proof would be that when Jesus shows up and speaks and performs miracles people become outright astonished.

Here are a few examples,

•**Mark 7:37** *"And were beyond measure astonished, saying, He hath done all things well: he maketh both the deaf to hear, and the dumb to speak."*

•**Luke 2:47** *"And all that heard him were astonished at his understanding and answers."*

•**Luke 4:32** *"And they were astonished at his doctrine: for his word was with power."*

So when Jesus shows up people are astonished. King Nebuchadnezzar was astonished and responded by changing a law. We must let the results of their uncompromised devotion get into us in a deep way that causes all compromise to disappear from our lives.

> Daniel 3:28-4:3 states, *"Then Nebuchadnezzar spoke, and said, Blessed be the God of Shadrach, Meshach, and Abednego, who hath sent his angel, and delivered his servants that trusted in him, and have changed the*

> *king's word, and yielded their bodies, that they might not serve nor worship any god, except their own God. Therefore I make a decree, That every people, nation, and language, which speak any thing amiss against the God of Shadrach, Meshach, and Abednego, shall be cut in pieces, and their houses shall be made a dunghill: because there is no other God that can deliver after this sort. Then the king promoted Shadrach, Meshach, and Abednego, in the province of Babylon. Nebuchadnezzar the king, unto all people, nations, and languages, that dwell in all the earth; Peace be multiplied unto you. I thought it good to show the signs and wonders that the high God hath wrought toward me. How great are his signs! And how mighty are his wonders! His kingdom is an everlasting kingdom, and his dominion is from generation to generation."*

There is a lot in this text. One of the keys to kingdom promotion is uncompromised devotion to the King. When King Jesus shows up, a revelation of his Kingdom is manifested. In Jesus' earthly ministry, his message was the Kingdom. When he shows up in the furnace in Babylon, the revelation King Nebuchadnezzar had was that there is a Kingdom greater than his. This revelation of the Kingdom causes him to change a law that went from prosecuting righteousness to executing unrighteousness. The beauty of Christ's supremacy is on the heart of the Father in this hour. The Father desires the nations to know that Jesus is Lord and that his Kingdom is above all other kingdoms.

Jesus' humanity is the mystery of his supremacy. It's incomprehensible to think someone can be fully God and fully man. If the Father doesn't reveal it, one truly can't understand it with the natural mind. The mystery of Christ is his divinity and humanity. The revealed mystery of Christ's identity is that he's fully God and fully man.

"For unto us a child is born, unto us a son is given: and the government shall be upon his shoulder: and his name shall be called Wonderful,

Counselor, The mighty God, The everlasting Father, The Prince of Peace." (Isaiah 9:6)

The child that is born is speaking of his *humanity* and the son that is given is speaking of his *deity*. The word wonderful in this verse in Hebrew means "miracle." His birth was miraculous because he was born of a virgin. His death was miraculous because he gave up the ghost, meaning no man took his life; he laid it down.

Jesus was manifested in the flesh and he was also born of a virgin according to the prophecy of Isaiah, and it's fulfillment in Matthew 1:23-25. He is the Son of Man, which means he must be born like a man would from the womb of a woman. He is also the Son of God, which means he was manifested in the flesh because he always existed. He is the Lamb slain from before the foundation of the world. This next verse speaks of his divinity.

"He that committeth sin is of the devil; for the devil sinneth from the beginning. For this purpose the Son of God was manifested, that he might destroy the works of the devil." (1 John 3:8)

This next verse speaks of his humanity. Isaiah 7:14 says, *"Therefore the Lord himself shall give you a sign; Behold, a virgin shall conceive, and bear a son, and shall call his name Immanuel."* Even when Mary was pregnant with him his divinity is revealed. Here is Elizabeth, John the Baptist's mother speaking about Jesus.

"And whence is this to me, that the mother of my Lord should come to me?" (Luke 1:43)

Here Jesus is called Lord even before he comes out of the womb. The reason being is because he truly was, is and always will be. His divinity was seen at his birth and his humanity was visible in his death. *Christ's supremacy is seen in the frailty of his humanity and the absolute authority of his divinity.* Jesus as a man was touched by our infirmities enough to heal them like only God could. He can give beauty for ashes because he is altogether lovely. The message of the Kingdom was Jesus' message meaning because we live in the

Kingdom our message is him. There is no kingdom without Jesus. We must never neglect the King when we are preaching or teaching on the Kingdom of God. In Jesus' earthly ministry, his supremacy is seen so clearly. Jesus turns water into wine; *the word impossible is not in his vocabulary.* He walks on water totally defying gravity. He is greater than the lack of wine or the law of gravity. He is above all created realties; he is the creator of all things.

"Behold, he that keepeth Israel shall neither slumber nor sleep." (Psalm 121:4)

Jesus was fully man so he had to sleep. He was also fully God so he could sleep in a storm! Jesus rebuked the storm and it stopped. He told the wind to stop and it did. He commanded demons to come out and they did. He healed and the dead He raised. There was no impossibility bigger than him. The true message of the Kingdom causes faith to arise and Jesus becomes bigger than anything we are up against. When he is on our side, him plus us is a majority. An amazing picture of Christ's supremacy is seen in the Gospel of John when Judas the betrayer and the soldiers go to the garden of Gethsemane to take Jesus into custody.

> *"Jesus therefore, knowing all things that should come upon him, went forth, and said unto them, Whom seek ye? They answered him, Jesus of Nazareth. Jesus saith unto them, I am he. And Judas also, which betrayed him, stood withthem. As soon then as he had said unto them, I am he, they went backward, and fell to the ground. Then asked he them again, Whom seek ye? And they said, Jesus of Nazareth. Jesus answered, I have told you that I am he: if therefore ye seek me, let these go their way: That the saying might be fulfilled, which he spake, Of them which thou gavest me have I lost none."* (John 18:4-9)

They came looking for Jesus and all ended up on their backs. Remember when Jesus said, "No man takes my life, I lay it down" he really meant it. Well that is a great illustration of the verse above.

The Increase of His Government

First he lays them down to show his sovereign power, and then he gives himself to them. Before he gives himself over to them he asks them while they are still in the floor. So who are you looking for? Jesus has the most amazing personality ever. There was about a hundred soldiers on the ground and Jesus asks them, *"Who are you looking for?"* That's so awesome. Many well-meaning misinformed teachers say that God doesn't violate man's free will. My question to them would be did those men ask to be knocked down when they stepped into the presence of a King un-invited? Here Christ's humanity, sovereignty and supremacy are all visible in this amazing scene from the gospel of John.

After Jesus puts himself into their hands; his physical suffering begins. His humanity was whipped and beaten to the point where he couldn't even carry his own cross.

"And as they led him away, they laid hold upon one Simon, a Cyrenian, coming out of the country, and on him they laid the cross, that he might bear it after Jesus." (Luke 23:26)

His humanity couldn't carry a cross but his deity made the decision to redeem mankind and that he did. So while Jesus is hanging there naked on a tree he says something profound.

"And when Jesus had cried with a loud voice, he said, Father, into thy hands I commend my spirit: and having said thus, he gave up the ghost." (Luke 23:46)

Remember Jesus said, *"no man takes his life I lay it down."* He was so human he could die. He was so God he could put his Spirit in the Father's hand as he hung naked from a tree outside of Jerusalem. Truly there is no one like him. After his resurrection he ate with his disciples, and even before his ascension he transcended time, space and matter when the doors of the house were shut and he appeared in the midst of his disciples. After forty days of teaching on the Kingdom of God he ascended to heaven to sit at God the Father's right hand until *"he makes his enemies his footstool."* (See Psalm 110:1 and Acts 2:35)

Adam LiVecchi

The simplicity of the message of the Kingdom is that Jesus is Lord. Doctrinally we know that but often experientially we don't. If our doctrine and experiences are not in alignment perhaps we may be double minded?

"And why call ye me, Lord, Lord, and do not the things which I say?" (Luke 6:46)

It appears here that Jesus desires that our statement of faith and lifestyle are in agreement with one another. The man who Jesus is talking to had sound doctrine but was deceived. His doctrine was true, but it wasn't true for him. He doctrinally knew Jesus was Lord, but his life didn't paint the same picture. There is no disobedience in the Kingdom. If we truly desire to live in the Kingdom, obedience is our only option. Often what most Charismatic/Pentecostal Christians call legalism God calls righteousness and holiness. True holiness just means that God is the only one we truly desire to please and that everything and everyone else is second place to Jesus. All authority has been given to Christ; therefore, he sent us. As we obey him, we re-present him to a world that is perishing. We represent him properly with power and character. His commands are to conform us into his image as our lives paint a picture of who God really is to the world.

CHAPTER 5

THE COMMANDS OF THE KINGDOM

The commands of the Kingdom are to make us like the King. When we obey his word, he manifests himself. As we learn to obey, we become conformed to the image of Christ. *As Jesus conforms us into his image, we are equipped to transform the world around us.* It's not enough to see someone come to church and pray a prayer; his or her whole life must be transformed by Jesus from the inside out. One of our greatest privileges is to partner with God in what he is doing in the earth. The gospel must advance at all costs. The gospel cost Jesus his life and for others to know him we must fully surrender our life to Jesus.

The Kingdom is an amazing place; because it's a reflection of the King. Let's look deep into Jesus' eyes for a moment.

"His head and his hairs were white like wool, as white as snow; and his eyes were as a flame of fire." (Revelation 1:14)

Our focus here is his eyes that are like flames of fire. His eyes burn with eternal love and supreme justice at the same time. His eyes and appearance put John the Revelator face down on the floor like a dead man. John ended up in the posture of worship. Another way to define worship is obedience. We can lie on the floor and worship and sing but our life must be a reflection of Jesus or we are religious hypocrites. Obeying Jesus' commands is what truly makes us true worshippers. Those are the kind of people that the Father is seeking. He is seeking people to be Jesus' reflection in the earth as they obey his commands and are transformed into his image.

"The statutes of the LORD are right, rejoicing the heart: the commandment of the LORD is pure, enlightening the eyes." (Psalm 19:8) God's word is to affect how we feel and how we see. In this verse there is some hidden wisdom. The phrase "enlightening the eyes" in Hebrew literally means, "to set on fire."

Jesus' commands make our eyes just like his. This is deeply profound but also very simple. The more simple God makes something the more responsible we are for what God has revealed. When we live in the Kingdom, we are to only let Jesus control how we feel and how we see. Our past failures and current circumstances cannot dictate how we feel or what we think. His commands train our hearts and minds to be just like his. *Living from God's perspective is so important we have been given the mind of Christ.*

The commandments of the Kingdom are found in Matthew 5:3-12.

> *Blessed are the poor in spirit: for theirs is the kingdom of heaven. Blessed are they that mourn: for they shall be comforted. Blessed are the meek: for they shall inherit the earth. Blessed are they which do hunger and thirst after righteousness: for they shall be filled. Blessed are the merciful: for they shall obtain mercy. Blessed are the pure in heart: for they shall see God. Blessed are the peacemakers: for they shall be called the children of God. Blessed are they which are persecuted for righteousness' sake: for theirs is the kingdom of heaven. Blessed are ye, when men shall revile you, and persecute you, and shall say all manner of evil against you falsely, for my sake. Rejoice, and be exceeding glad: for great is your*

> *reward in heaven: for so persecuted they the prophets which were before you.*

These verses perfectly describe how Jesus lived. Life comes from his mouth because he is God and also because he lived what he spoke. When we are hypocrites, there is no life or power on our words because we are not living what we are speaking. To be certain that these verses are commands let's continue to see what Jesus says in that very same chapter just a few verses later. Remember we don't interpret the Bible the Bible interprets the Bible.

"Whosoever therefore shall break one of these least commandments, and shall teach men so, he shall be called the least in the kingdom of heaven: but whosoever shall do and teach them, the same shall be called great in the kingdom of heaven." (Matthew 5:19)

So in this verse we learn that the beatitudes are not suggestions but commands. Those commands conform us to the image of Christ. As we obey his commands, his light shines through us and people around us can come out of darkness into his marvelous light. God in his infinite wisdom has designed his light to shine through us; all we must do is obey. In the Kingdom obedience is the only option.

"Let your light so shine before men, that they may see your good works, and glorify your Father which is in heaven." (Matthew 5:16)

Something must be done for light to shine. It's not enough to just pray that light shines, but we must obey what God says so he can become visible to those who don't know him through our good works. If the gospel we preach is good news, than there must be some corresponding good works or we are preaching the gospel but not actually walking in truth. When we walk in truth others can experience what we say. The gospel must be demonstrated, not just talked about but it also must be lived out.

In the book of Daniel, there is a prophecy about the saints possessing the Kingdom. Daniel 7:18 says, *"But the saints of the most High shall take the kingdom, and possess the kingdom for ever, even for ever and ever."* Daniel prophesied this and wrote it down so we could read it. Jesus lived it out and taught us how by setting an example for us.

"Blessed are the poor in spirit: for theirs is the kingdom of heaven." (Matthew 5:3)

We possess the Kingdom by being poor in Spirit. As we recognize our need for Jesus, he becomes immediately available to and for us. This is true biblically, historically and presently. Have you ever heard someone tell you that before they were Christian they spoke to God and said "if" you are real speak to me or do this? If we continue to listen to them that story usually leads to their testimony of salvation. When we recognize our need for Jesus, then he comes walking right into our brokenness, sin and lack. We possess the Kingdom by being poor in Spirit. To be rich toward God we must be poor in Spirit. There are two scriptures that illustrate what being poor in Spirit looks like really well. The first one is when Jesus was speaking to his disciples. John 15:5 says, *"I am the vine, ye are the branches: He that abideth in me, and I in him, the same bringeth forth much fruit: for without me ye can do nothing."* The revelation that we can do nothing without Jesus is elementary. Jesus didn't just tell us this; he lived it out continually and also put language to it in his own life and ministry.

"Then answered Jesus and said unto them, Verily, verily, I say unto you, The Son can do nothing of himself, but what he seeth the Father do: for what things so ever he doeth, these also doeth the Son likewise." (John 5:19)

This is what it looks like to be poor in Spirit. Being poor in Spirit doesn't mean we don't do anything. It means our affections are set above so we are attentive to God and therefore we see and hear that which he wants to say and do and we then partner with him. In the doing so, our light shines before men as we set our affections on God. Our affections are clearly seen in our actions. Paul the apostle also puts language to being poor in Spirit.

"I can do all things through Christ which strengtheneth me." (Philippians 4:13)

After we realize we can do nothing without Jesus, he then reveals to us we can do all things through him. Christ strengthens us to obey his commands, not just to go to church when we are tired because of a hard week at work. Someone who is poor in Spirit is someone who is not afraid to confess their sin or even admit when and why they are wrong. If we are going to live from God's resources, we have to declare total bankruptcy of the flesh and it's lusts.

Being poor in Spirit means we put no confidence in the flesh. If we put no confidence in the flesh then we can be lead by the Spirit of God. The Spirit cannot lead us if we have confidence in the flesh. Many Christians need what I call the crippling experience. Before God changed Jacob's name to Israel, he was crippled. Jacob wrestled all night with a man. The man touched Jacob's hip and it came out of place, meaning he walked with a limp. (See Genesis 32:24-32) It was then when his name was changed from Jacob the deceiver to Israel the prince. Everyone in the Kingdom walks with a limp. I am certainly not speaking of a physical malady but a Spiritual understanding of their desperate need for Jesus. Being poor in Spirit means we live by every word that proceeds from the mouth of God. Many of us haven't learned to listen enough to truly live by every word that God is speaking. However, I believe the Father desires a people to give their full attention and allegiance to his Son Jesus through the operation of his Holy Spirit. These kind of people are called true worshippers, and the Father is seeking them out in this hour. As we seek first the Kingdom of God, he will search us out and make us like him.

On Jesus' physical body he bears our proof of purchase on his back, side, hands and feet. By being poor in Spirit, we have access to what Jesus has purchased for us when he gave us himself. He has our proof of purchase on him; therefore, we are his inheritance. When someone purchases something, they are usually given a receipt especially if it is a significant purchase. A receipt would be called a proof of purchase. There is proof for all those who truly posses the Kingdom of God in the same way a tree is known by its fruit. The evidence that we have received what Jesus has freely given us when he gave us the kingdom is simply bearing fruit and being persecuted for it. The enemy only persecutes what is a threat to him.

"Yea, and all that will live godly in Christ Jesus shall suffer persecution." (2 Timothy 3:12)

The only way to live in the kingdom is by the King's standards, which is obviously godly if it's the Kingdom of God. Perhaps Paul gets this truth from the truth himself in, Matthew 5:10 which says, *"Blessed are they which are persecuted for righteousness' sake: for theirs is the kingdom of heaven."* Here the persecuted possess the kingdom that Daniel prophesied about. It's important that we see the word of the Lord. Suffering and persecution is definitely part of the Gospel Jesus preached. If we possess the Kingdom and are preaching the Gospel of the Kingdom, we will suffer persecution. Even if we are just living godly we still will be persecuted for righteousness' sake. Saying what's right will create opposition but doing what is right will bring persecution. The enemy first tries to silence the prophetic voice and in doing so his intention is to shut down and stop the apostolic community from advancing the Kingdom. Remember nothing in the Kingdom happens without declaration, if the voice can be silenced then the movement can be stopped.

If we are going to be people of the Kingdom who obey the King, we will have both blessing and persecution. It's not one or the other it's both. If there is no opposition against us, are we really moving forward? When someone is living in compromise, there is nothing really opposing him or her because he or she isn't going anywhere. We will have times of adversity and also times of prosperity. Both adversity and prosperity will show us who we really are and what we truly value. *When pressure comes on us we see what is really in us.* This also happens with gold. It's the fire that shows what the gold is really worth. In Matthew 11:12, Jesus said, *"And from the days of John the Baptist until now the kingdom of heaven suffereth violence, and the violent take it by force."* Obedience to him will lead to both suffering for him and reigning with him. Paul the Apostle also knew this really well.

"If we suffer, we shall also reign with him: if we deny him, he also will deny us." (2 Timothy 2:12)

Training for reigning is suffering. We learn obedience through suffering, or real obedience leads to suffering. In our time of testing or trials, we must be obedient in spite of what may happen to us. We go through this adversity ourselves first so we can lead others through correctly. After we have set our hearts to follow Jesus and obey his word, we then become responsible to teach and lead others. In the Kingdom the only form of leadership is by example. In church you hear all kinds of foolishness like, "I am not called to evangelism." What they are really saying is either I don't know how to share my faith or I don't love Jesus enough to want to. If we are Christians, we are called to evangelism. If we are not called to evangelism, we are simply not Christians. Remember every fruit bearing seed reproduces itself. The fruit of a Christian is not going to church on Sunday or even the tithe; the fruit of a Christian is another Christian.

"He that is not with me is against me: and he that gathereth not with me scattereth." (Luke 11:23)

Jesus seems to be pretty clear here. If we are not pulling people into the Kingdom, we are pushing them into hell. Therefore, if we are "chosen" to go to heaven we are called to bring people with us. It's pretty simple. Religion always tries to complicate what Jesus has made simple.

Jesus is so concerned about our lifestyle that he gave his life so we would have eternal life. His intention is that our lives would be fully yielded to him in the Kingdom. *Lifestyle is very important to Jesus. Before he gave the disciples a statement of faith or taught them how to pray, he commanded them how to live.* Jesus taught them how to live in such a way that their light would shine and through their light or him in them they would become hidden in him and the Father would become visible through them. Jesus didn't just teach them his statement of faith; he commanded them to be it. Here are two things we are called to be if we are truly citizens from above.

"Ye are the salt of the earth: but if the salt have lost his savor, wherewith shall it be salted? it is thenceforth good for nothing, but to be cast out, and to be trodden under foot of men. Ye are the light of the world. A city that is set on an hill cannot be hid." (Matthew 5:13-14)

Salt is for preservation and light is for revelation. We are the preservation for the planet and the revelation of God's Son here on earth. Our lives must always point to Jesus if we call ourselves Christians. Jesus prophesied the disciples were light even before they were shining. Prophecy clothes us with identity, meaning we are who God says that we are by the grace of God because he said so. We are to be a revelation of Jesus on the earth, simply because he lives in us and we live and move and have our being in him. As we obey the Gospel, we become a sign that points directly to Jesus. Obedience to the gospel is what gives us the privilege and responsibility to preach it.

"Whosoever therefore shall break one of these least commandments, and shall teach men so, he shall be called the least in the kingdom of heaven: but whosoever shall do and teach them, the same shall be called great in the kingdom of heaven." (Matthew 5:19)

Learning doesn't give us authority to teach; doing what Jesus has told us to do does. In America and the developed world especially, the church is so fascinated with learning often it forgets the doing part. It's important to understand that action solidifies learning. The proper order in the kingdom is to do then teach; however, most leaders are teaching but not doing. This is called hypocrisy and it's time to *"repent because the Kingdom of God is at hand."* The gospel of the Kingdom gives birth to the church and the epistles facilitate the growth and health of the church through the Holy Spirit. Remember the church is not the Kingdom; it's in the Kingdom. Jesus taught us to be the church and Paul taught us how to do church. Jesus releases the substance and Paul brings the structure. For too long there has been a structure with no substance. For a very long time people have been satisfied with a form of godliness with no real power to change lives, let alone the world we live in. Jesus taught his disciples to live in such a way that when they prayed the Father listened. He taught them humility, which would make them absolutely irresistible to the Father. What he commanded them then, he still requires from us today. This is only possible through the Holy Spirit that raised Jesus from the death who lives in us.

Deception is not just false doctrine; deception can also be someone who has sound doctrine and doesn't do anything about what Jesus has commanded them to do.

"But be ye doers of the word, and not hearers only, deceiving your own selves." (James 1:22)

If we just keep listening every Sunday and never do anything about it on Monday we can become completely deceived even with sound doctrine. Most people have enough truth on their statement of faith to not know they are truly deceived by a lifestyle of hearing and never doing anything about it. *I am not belittling the necessity for sound doctrine because there is no false doctrine in the Kingdom of God.* I am simply saying our lifestyle and doctrine must line up, the same way we must have character and power; it's not one or the other it's both. People do not want to hear our truth if they don't see our integrity. It was Daniel's integrity to the truth, which made the truth visible to Babylon. He didn't compromise God's word and God truly was a shield to Daniel in the lion's den because he walked uprightly. Here obedience brought danger but God brought deliverance. Remember the Kingdom of heaven suffers violence and the violent take it by force.

CHAPTER 6

PRAY THE KINGDOM

We have just received commandments that will conform us into the image of Christ. Jesus taught his disciples and us to live the Kingdom. *The commands of Matthew 5:3-12 are what form Christ in us as we obey him. They are commandments not suggestions.* We grow in him as we obey him; the same way he grows in us as we obey him. Jesus has just taught us to be irresistible to the Father through obeying his commands.

Humility can only be seen through our obedience. Living in subjection to Christ is being humble before almighty God. Being humble is not speaking with a soft voice and calling people brother or sister before we address them by their name. When we are humble or poor in spirit, there is something we quickly come to understand. *The poor in Spirit understand their desperate need to hear from and pray to God and therefore possess the Kingdom of God. The poor in Spirit possess what cannot be bought with money.*

Before Jesus taught the disciples to pray "thy kingdom come" he taught them to "live thy kingdom come." It's obvious that true discipleship is not in how much you pray or say the truth, but how much your life reflects the truth through everything you believe, pray, do and say. Roughly 700 B.C there was a prophecy about the Kingdom of God. Jesus aims his prayer at a prophetic word; he inspired Isaiah to speak about 730 years prior to him teaching the disciples to pray.

> *"For unto us a child is born, unto us a son is given: and the government shall be upon his shoulder: and his name shall be called Wonderful, Counselor, The mighty God, The everlasting Father, The Prince of Peace.* ***Of the increase of his government and peace there shall be no end****, upon the throne of David, and upon his kingdom, to order it, and to establish it with judgment and with justice from henceforth even forever. The zeal of the LORD of hosts will perform this."* (Isaiah 9:6-7)

My focus is on the bold words. Jesus' kingdom or government is continually and eternally increasing. Even though Jesus doesn't change; his Kingdom still never ceases to increase. While blood was dripping out of his body, while he hung naked on a tree, his Kingdom was still increasing. When he was dead for three days and his body was lying in a tomb, his word was alive and it was holding all things together, and his kingdom was still increasing. If you believe one thing I write believe this, *"There is no one like Jesus."* Through Jesus' teaching, prayer and prophecy come together. Jesus is initiating this through his wisdom. Jesus is the alpha and the omega and the beginning and the ending. All accurate prophecy does is reveals Jesus who knows the end from the beginning. Signs point to Jesus, wonders cause us to be fascinated with Jesus and prophecy reveals and points to Jesus. Revelation 19:10 b says, *"Worship God: for the testimony of Jesus is the spirit of prophecy."*

Jesus teaches his disciples to pray the Kingdom because he has prophesied that it would continually increase. Both Jesus and John the Baptist started off their ministries with the very same phrase. In Matthew 3:2, John the Baptist said, *"And saying, Repent ye: for the kingdom of heaven is at hand."* In Matthew 4:17, Jesus said, *"From that time Jesus began to preach, and to say, Repent: for the kingdom of heaven is at hand."* So Jesus teaches his disciples to pray *"thy kingdom come"* in the context of first telling them how to live it. Before we go into the Lord's Prayer let's see what Jesus said before he teaches them to pray.

> *"Therefore when thou doest thine alms, do not sound a trumpet before thee, as the hypocrites do in the synagogues and in the streets, that they may have glory of men. Verily I say unto you, They have their reward. But when thou doest alms, let not thy left hand know what thy right hand doeth: That thine alms may be in secret: and thy Father which seeth in secret himself shall reward thee openly."* (Matthew 6:2-4)

Jesus didn't say *"if"* you **give**, he said when you give. Jesus taught them to give before he even told them what to ask for. He is so concerned with our heart motivations and our lifestyle. Jesus teaches his followers how to live and with what motivation to give before he even teaches them to ask for anything. The reason he does this is because he himself said to Paul the Apostle, *"It is more blessed to give than to receive"*, see Acts 20:35.

Jesus continues his discourse on the kingdom lifestyle; some people call it Christianity 101. What we call it doesn't really matter; the real issue is do we live it.

> *"And when thou prayest, thou shalt not be as the hypocrites are: for they love to pray standing in the synagogues and in the corners of the streets, that they may be seen of men. Verily I say unto you, They have their reward. But thou, when thou prayest, enter into thy closet, and when thou hast shut thy door, pray to thy Father which is in secret; and thy Father which seeth in secret shall reward thee openly. But when ye pray, use not vain repetitions, as the heathen do: for they think that they shall be heard for their much speaking."* (Matthew 6:5-7)

Here Jesus is telling his disciples the proper place and proper motivation to pray. Again he said when you pray, not if you pray.

Then Jesus goes into what many people know as the Lord's Prayer or the Our Father. Matthew 6:9 says, *"After this manner therefore pray ye: Our Father which art in heaven, Hallowed be thy name."* Often you hear people say this was the first time God was mentioned as Father. Unfortunately that isn't true although, it sounds good. Jesus was referred to as the Son of David; this term identifies that Jesus was the Messiah, and he is the fulfillment of the Prophecy in Isaiah 11:1 which states, *"And there shall come forth a rod out of the stem of Jesse, and a Branch shall grow out of his roots."* Jesse was David's Father. What's awesome is that Jesus was the Son of David but also the everlasting Father to a whole new creation of men and women who would be born again or born from above. Before Jesus came and put on flesh and said, "I am the light of the world." David said, Psalm 27:1 which says, *"The LORD is my light and my salvation; whom shall I fear? the LORD is the strength of my life; of whom shall I be afraid?"* David had a profound relationship with God; he was even called a man after God's own heart. Let's examine one of King David's prayers.

> *"Wherefore David blessed the LORD before all the congregation: and David said, Blessed be thou, LORD God of Israel our father, for ever and ever. Thine, O LORD, is the greatness, and the power, and the glory, and the victory, and the majesty: for all that is in the heaven and in the earth is thine; thine is the kingdom, O LORD, and thou art exalted as head above all. Both riches and honor come of thee, and thou reignest over all; and in thine hand is power and might; and in thine hand it is to make great, and to give strength unto all. Now therefore, our God, we thank thee, and praise thy glorious name."* (1 Chronicles 29:10-12)

In this prayer, David mentions God as Father. We also later see *"thine is the kingdom"* also appears in the Lord's Prayer. In the Old Testament David was the high standard. God even showed mercy to people because of them being related to him.

"Notwithstanding in thy days I will not do it for David thy father's sake: but I will rend it out of the hand of thy son." (1 Kings 11:12)

God uses David's life as the high watermark so to speak because Jesus hadn't manifested in the flesh. So the revelation that only David had then everyone has now because Jesus came in the flesh and reconciled us back to God by the shedding of His blood. We live in amazing times. The least in the Kingdom is greater than John the Baptist. The shedding of Jesus' blood has truly transformed the standard.

In Matthew 6, Jesus lays out the standard. God is our Father; he is in heaven. His name is holy, and he is to be feared. *The fear of the Lord causes us to run to him and not from him.* The fear of the Lord is a key to having our prayers heard, we see this truth in the life of Jesus.

"Who in the days of his flesh, when he had offered up prayers and supplications with strong crying and tears unto him that was able to save him from death, and was heard in that he feared." (Hebrews 5:7)

In the Kingdom, the king is to be loved and feared. The fear of the Lord is the key to the Lord hearing us and us hearing him. Jesus taught us to boldly approach the throne and ask "thy kingdom come." Boldly approaching the throne is asking God for what he has told us to ask him for so that he will do what he already said he would do. Jesus is telling us how to approach God and what to ask of him when we do. To fully understand the prayer *"thy kingdom come on earth as it is in heaven"* we would have to do an extensive Bible study of heaven and then we still would not know it all because his government or kingdom is ever increasing. There are some really simple things that are in heaven that are not on the earth such as God the Father and Jesus sitting at his right hand. There is peace that is uninterrupted in heaven. Everything in heaven is alive, worship never stops, and there is the perfect administration of authority. There is no sickness, no disease, no crime, and no evil music. There are no boring church services. The list could go on and on but I think you get the point. By praying, "thy kingdom come on earth as it is in heaven" we are simply inviting Jesus' righteousness, peace and joy to fill the earth. In this prayer we are partnering with prophecy as well. The Bible says "the knowledge of God's glory will cover the earth like waters cover the sea." Praying thy Kingdom come - is asking God for this word to be manifested. Glory is the atmosphere of royalty. When the Kingdom comes glory is manifest and Jesus receives the honor that he is due. That is the Fathers goal. The Son's glory is the Father's primary ambition.

Jesus continues to teach his disciples how to pray. Matthew 6:11-13 says, *"Give us this day our daily bread. And forgive us our debts, as we forgive our debtors. And lead us not into temptation, but deliver us from evil: For thine is the kingdom, and the power, and the glory, forever. Amen."* Jesus is telling them to ask for what they need by saying give us our daily bread. Learning to ask for what we need is how we truly learn to trust God as we walk by faith. A life of true discipleship requires trusting God daily, whether it's for food that day or for the money to pay for a huge church building. Serving and following Jesus will always keep you in a place of utter dependency on the Father. Even if one becomes wealthy as a Christian they will need to utterly depend on God to show them how to steward that wealth wisely. We will talk about Kingdom investing later in the book. Forgiving people of their debts, means if people owe you money let it go. It means if someone sins against you let it go. If we don't forgive the only person we are really holding back is our self. Here Jesus is teaching us to live with a predisposition to forgive others even if they don't say they are sorry. We have received a ministry of reconciliation that is manifested through forgiveness. Jesus said "whoever sins you forgive I will forgive." He wasn't saying that we could pick and choose whom we can forgive or who will go to heaven or hell. He was saying that if you forgive someone for sinning against you he would not hold it against him or her on judgment day. Because you have chose to forgive he then forgets because you forgave. That is good news.

Lead us not into temptation, is one of the least prayed parts of this prayer. A lot of Christian leaders fall into sin because of failure to pray this prayer. When we are poor in spirit, we are aware of our weakness and our desperate need for God to lead us in the way we should go and keep us from the way we should not go. We must pray this prayer daily because temptations are everywhere. Before we had to go looking for them now they pop up on our phones and on computers even when we are not looking for them.

Let's see why Jesus taught them to pray, *"lead me not into temptation."*

> Luke 22:40-46 says, *"And when he was at the place, he said unto them, Pray that ye enter not into temptation. And he was withdrawn from them about a stone's cast, and kneeled down, and prayed, Saying, Father, if thou be willing, remove this cup from me: nevertheless not my will, but thine, be done. And there appeared an angel unto him from heaven, strengthening him. And being in an agony he prayed more earnestly: and his sweat was as it were great drops of blood falling down to the ground. And when he rose up from prayer, and was come to his disciples, he found them sleeping for sorrow, And said unto them, Why sleep ye? rise and pray, lest ye enter into temptation."*

Jesus warned them but they didn't have ears to hear. He told them to pray that they wouldn't enter into temptation and then they fell asleep. All of them except John the Revelator ended up betraying Jesus. Only John showed up at the foot of the cross. Perhaps John prayed, *"lead me not into temptation."* Whether he did or not Jesus warned them to pray and that warning is for us too. How many people, families, churches and ministries are led into temptation simply because they don't ask God to "lead me not into temptation?" There are many needless casualties because this prayer is not prayed.

The last part of the Lord's Prayer is a revelation of the Father. The prayer begins and ends with a revelation of the Father.

"After this manner therefore pray ye: Our Father which art in heaven, Hallowed be thy name." (Matthew 6:13)

"And lead us not into temptation, but deliver us from evil: For thine is the kingdom, and the power, and the glory, for ever. Amen." (Matthew 6:9)

Jesus' goal in prayer is to reveal the Father to us. Before Philip asked Jesus to "show us the Father" Jesus was already revealing him. Prayer should begin and end with a revelation of Our Father who is in heaven whose name is Holy. He is the kingdom, power and glory forever. Remember Jesus came to reveal the Father, and his message was the Kingdom.

Jesus first taught the disciples how to live. Then he began to teach them the whens of Christianity. He taught them when you give and when you pray and when you fast. He then teaches the Lord's Prayer. Directly after the Lord's Prayer, he teaches them about forgiveness. He tells them that "if they don't forgive people the Father won't forgive them." That is a very strong sobering reality. Many people are delusional. They think they have an authentic relationship with God, but when they have unforgiveness towards someone biblically they have NO relationship with God! Our relationship with God is strictly based on forgiveness; if we don't give any; then we don't receive any. After that Jesus teaches them about fasting. I am including this in the kingdom prayer because the prayer was taught in the context of how to live.

"But thou, when thou fastest, anoint thine head, and wash thy face; That thou appear not unto men to fast, but unto thy Father which is in secret: and thy Father, which seeth in secret, shall reward thee openly." (Matthew 6:17-18)

Again he said when you **fast**, not if you fast. Fasting is as much a part of the Christian life as praying and giving. These are the three whens of the kingdom. They are: give, pray and fast. These are crucial elements to the Christian life. What we gain with passion, we maintain with discipline and increase through wisdom. Jesus went from teaching about forgiveness to teaching about fasting. This is pretty interesting. I think there is a reason why. Fasting is about denying our flesh and so is forgiveness. Sometimes when someone wrongs us we feel we have the right to be angry, but in reality we are commanded to forgive. Our feelings mean nothing and our faith has to believe God enough to simply obey him. This is similar to our natural body; it wants and deserves food but sometimes it's just isn't going to get any for a while. This does something on the inside of a person that is priceless. If we can teach our body to submit, we can also teach our feelings to submit. In the Kingdom of God, the Jesus within is Lord. Therefore our feelings and circumstances must not rule us. Idolatry is not just bowing down to idols, its also being held hostage by our feelings, emotions or even desires.

Remember there is only one Lord in the kingdom, and it's Jesus. *In the kingdom of God there is no unforgiveness.* There is a strong connection between, faith, fasting and forgiveness and if we are going to see "thy kingdom come on earth as it is in heaven" in our lives, families, churches and communities then we will have to understand this connection.

> *Then said he unto the disciples, It is impossible but that offences will come: but woe unto him, through whom they come! It were better for him that a millstone were hanged about his neck, and he cast into the sea, than that he should offend one of these little ones. Take heed to yourselves: If thy brother trespass against thee, rebuke him; and if he repent, forgive him. And if he trespass against thee seven times in a day, and seven times in a day turn again to thee, saying, I repent; thou shalt forgive him. And the apostles said unto the Lord, Increase our faith.* (Luke 17:1-5)

When Jesus tells his disciples they need to forgive each other, they ask him for more faith. The only time they asked for more faith is when he told them they needed to forgive each other. Here we see that faith and forgiveness are tied together.
Here is the faith and fasting connection.

> Luke 17:15-21 says, *"Lord, have mercy on my son: for he is lunatick, and sore vexed: for ofttimes he falleth into the fire, and oft into the water. And I brought him to thy disciples, and they could not cure him. Then Jesus answered and said, O faithless and perverse generation, how long shall I be with you? how long shall I suffer you? bring him hither to me. And Jesus rebuked the devil; and he departed out of him: and the child was cured from that very hour. Then came the disciples to Jesus apart, and said, Why could not we cast him out? And Jesus said unto them, Because of your unbelief: for verily I say unto you, If ye have faith as a grain of mustard seed, ye shall say unto this mountain, Remove hence to yonder place; and it shall remove; and nothing shall be impossible unto you. Howbeit this kind goeth not out but by prayer and fasting."*

The disciples couldn't cast out a Spirit of Lunacy; therefore, Jesus asked them where was their faith. It was because of their unbelief that they couldn't do it. Then Jesus comes to their rescue just like he does to ours when we are not prepared for the circumstances that arise in our life. Then he gives them the key to this one. A lifestyle of prayer and fasting will lead to an increase of faith and power. Praying and fasting doesn't change God's mind; it changes ours. Fasting builds faith; faith releases people from the demonic, and faith also forgiveness people even when they don't say they are sorry. Jesus rebuked the disciples for not being the church. Often we hear people rebuke people for not going to church or even being late to church, but Jesus rebuked them for not being the church. One of keys to seeing the Kingdom manifest in our lives, families, churches and communities are, **giving, praying, fasting, and forgiving**. These are the ingredients that make a world changer. The Jesus who gave himself for us also forgave those who didn't say they were sorry. He prayed and fasted and brought the kingdom everywhere he went. If we are his followers, we to must do the same.

CHAPTER 7

SEEKING THE KINGDOM

Growing up in church and in a good Christian home with amazing parents, I often heard people say, *"Seek first the Kingdom of God and his righteousness and all these things shall be added unto you."* I even knew the song they made about that verse. However, in all my years of Christianity, church and conferences I have never once heard someone explain what that verse is actually saying. I am going to endeavor to explain what it means and how we are to apply this command to our everyday lives.

*"I Jesus have sent mine angel to testify unto you these things in the churches. **I am the root and the offspring of David**, and the bright and morning star."* (Revelation 22:16)

I am focusing on the bold words. This statement would be similar to when Jesus said, *"Before Abraham was I am."* Here he is revealing his eternal existence. It's important to see the connection between Jesus and David. The last way Jesus revealed himself in the scriptures is when he said, *"I am the root and the offspring of David."* It is important to Jesus for us to know this. Therefore, it must be important to us. What matters to him should matter to us especially if we call Jesus Lord. Seeking the Kingdom first means Jesus is our first priority. Jesus taught us to live the kingdom in Matthew 5, to pray the kingdom in Matthew 6 and then he goes on to say at the end of Matthew 6 seek the kingdom first. It's pretty evident that Jesus is pretty serious about the kingdom of God. Here is a small progression that we should remember: *live, pray and seek the kingdom.*

David said something similar in concept. Psalms 27:4 says, *"One thing have I desired of the LORD, that will I seek after; that I may dwell in the house of the LORD all the days of my life, to behold the beauty of the LORD, and to enquire in his temple."* We must pursue what we desire if we hope to attain it. Many people are waiting on God but in reality he's actually waiting on us. Praying *"thy kingdom come"* is not enough. We must seek after what we are asking God for. It's like someone praying for a job and staying home and waiting until someone calls or e-mails them. If you want a job call places, fill out applications online and ask to speak to management in person. If you want something, you must go after it. When a believer stops fighting the good fight of faith they usually stop going after what they are asking God for and become passive instead of perseverant. Some would say you need to be patient and that's true, but *perseverance is only patience in motion*. We must be patient while waiting for the suddenly of God to break into our life, but we must persevere until God breaks in. Jesus telling us to seek what he told us to pray for is what real intercession looks like. *Prayer without action is not intersession; it's only a vain repetition at best.*

Matthew 6:33-34 says, *"But seek ye first the kingdom of God, and his righteousness; and all these things shall be added unto you. Take therefore no thought for the morrow: for the morrow shall take thought for the things of itself. Sufficient unto the day is the evil thereof."* Obeying Jesus' teachings must be our very first priority if we are going to seek first his kingdom and his righteousness. Our priorities must be his. In and of ourselves we can't do this; we need his help. When Jesus comes to live inside of us his properties are who we really are, meaning we become like him because he is living inside of us by faith. The enemy doesn't want us to know this, so he continually attacks our identity. Christ is our identity;

he purchased us from death and hell into light and life. Jesus came to earth and gave himself; he had no earthly citizenship so we can have a heavenly citizenship. As citizens of another world we must seek first his kingdom.

"We love him, because he first loved us." (1 John 4:19)

We love him because he first loved us; his first love towards us is what empowers us to seek the kingdom first. If we are going to seek first the kingdom of God today, we can't worry about tomorrow. *In the kingdom of God there are no worries.* If we want to be useful to God today we can't be fretting about yesterday or worried about tomorrow. To live a kingdom life we must be present in the *"now."*

What seeking the kingdom of God first really looks like is "bringing our whole existence under Jesus' wise and righteous leadership." This must be done in proper order. Seeking the kingdom first means it starts with us. As Jesus continues the Sermon on the Mount he said something that helps us to seek the kingdom first.

> *"And why beholdest thou the mote that is in thy brother's eye, but considerest not the beam that is in thine own eye? Or how wilt thou say to thy brother, Let me pull out the mote out of thine eye; and, behold, a beam is in thine own eye? Thou hypocrite, first cast out the beam out of thine own eye; and then shalt thou see clearly to cast out the mote out of thy brother's eye."* (Matthew 7: 3-5)

If we desire to seek first the kingdom of God and his righteousness, we can't focus on other people's problems. One day as I was praying Jesus said to me, *"If you took the log out of your eye you would be able to see me."* Ouch that hurt, but it also rearranged my priorities that were out of order. So you have a man with a big problem focusing on someone with a smaller problem. Here Jesus tells the man focusing on the other man's problems to deal with his log and then help his brother with his little speck. We must allow God to deal with us before we go around trying to deal with the world. The wood in the eye can really obstruct our vision. If we are going to be seeking the kingdom, we need clear spiritual sight. The man with out of order priorities focusing on someone else's weakness is actually a blind hypocrite. If we were honest with ourselves, we need to be vaccinated from the "log syndrome" if we are going to seek first the kingdom of God. In order to seek properly we need to see clearly. Once I prayed *"Lord Jesus, Rip the log out of my eye; whack me on the head with it and give me a heart and a mind transplant so I focus on you alone."* You can pray that prayer if you want. I dare you to. I am not sure how theologically correct it is, but it changed my life and continues to as I learn to take my eyes off myself and people and keep them on Jesus. If our eyes are on man when that man falls we will fall too, but if our eyes are on Jesus we will be able to run with perseverance.

As I mentioned earlier, when you want something bad enough you go after it whole heartedly, which means you don't take no for an answer. When a mother loses her child in the mall, she doesn't just stop looking for the child; she looks until she finds the child. That is the attitude we must have as we seek Jesus' leadership in our lives. We are not actually seeking Jesus because he is not hiding from us. We are seeking to administer his will to our lives and this planet.

> *"Ask, and it shall be given you; seek, and ye shall find; knock, and it shall be opened unto you: For every one that asketh receiveth; and he that seeketh findeth; and to him that knocketh it shall be opened."*
> (Matthew 7:7-8)

Here we see a progression of seeking. Progressions are very important to understand because the kingdom is continually increasing. Let's say I am looking for my brother Aaron. So I go in the kitchen and ask my mother, "Mother-dearest where is Aaron?" She replies, "Adam I am not sure. I know he is home because his car is here." So I go downstairs to where he lifts weights and practices the electric guitar. As I go downstairs seeking to find my brother, I realize he is not there. Then I go back upstairs and walk through the kitchen and up another small flight of stairs. Now I begin knocking on his door and as I knock he says, "Who is it?" and I say, "Adam" and he says, "Come in." This is a very practical picture of the verse above. Here I (Adam) was determined to find my brother and so I searched until I found him. We ask to receive, seek to find and knock until we get an answer. Faith asks and receives or asks until it receives, seeks until it finds and knocks until the door is answered. There are some things in the Kingdom that will only happen by persevering. Perseverance is faith in motion until it crosses the finish line. There are certain things that we just receive and there are other things that we press in and contend for until a breakthrough comes. We need discernment to understand which is necessary in the season we are in.

In all reality if we are going to seek first the kingdom of God whole heartedly there are things we must do and other things we must not do. Jesus makes it very clear when he tells us what we must do. He does that in Matthew 5 and 6 in a remarkably clear way. Paul the Apostle makes it very clear what we should not do if we desire the kingdom.

> *"Now the works of the flesh are manifest, which are these; Adultery, fornication, uncleanness, lasciviousness, Idolatry, witchcraft, hatred, variance, emulations, wrath, strife, seditions, heresies, Envyings, murders, drunkenness, revellings, and such like: of the which I tell you before, as I have also told you in time past, that they which do such things shall not inherit the kingdom of God."* (Galatians 5:19-21)

This is pretty simple and self-explanatory. In the kingdom there is one Lord, and He is Jesus. If we want to seek the Kingdom, we can't seek to gratify the lusts of the flesh. We cannot be slaves to sin in a kingdom where there is no sin. There may be sin in the church, or in me or in you but in the kingdom there is none. Seeking the kingdom first and his righteousness means that we obey Jesus no matter what. Above all things that is what the Holy

Spirit inside us desires. Jesus never grieved the Holy Spirit once. The Holy Spirit loves to make us obedient to Jesus because that is what really pleases the Father. It also pleases the Father to give us the kingdom. Jesus lived in perfect relation with his Father who is our Father because of him. He knew the Fathers heart because he was committed to his will even unto death. The commitment we have will determine the revelation we walk in. When Jesus said "repent the Kingdom of God is at hand" he said that knowing it was the Fathers pleasure to give us the Kingdom.

"But rather seek ye the kingdom of God; and all these things shall be added unto you. Fear not, little flock; for it is your Father's good pleasure to give you the kingdom." (Luke 12:31-32)

In very simple terms, seeking the kingdom first is really just living to please the Father just as Jesus did. We don't earn the kingdom because Jesus paid for it. It cost him everything so he can give it to us freely. It's free to receive the kingdom. However, we will pay a dear price to seek after it, press into it and advance it here on the earth.

Pressing into the kingdom is seeking the kingdom of God in a more fervent and persistent way. As we mature we don't only seek the kingdom we press into it. The more we press into it the more the king overflows onto the world around us. If we are filled with the Holy Spirit, we will naturally overflow onto the world around us. Peter is a great example of what happens when we press into the kingdom. He pressed into the kingdom in such a way that the kingdom of God leaked out of him onto the sick in the streets where he walked. Paul is also another great example. The sweat from his brow got on a handkerchief and was taken to the demonized and they were set free. Both of these men show the possibilities of what a life can produce when it is fully yield to Jesus and fully committed to the advancement of his kingdom.

CHAPTER 8

PREACHING AND DEMONSTRATING THE KINGDOM

1 Corinthians 2:4 says, *"And my speech and my preaching was not with enticing words of man's wisdom, but in demonstration of the Spirit and of power."* Preaching the kingdom must be accompanied with demonstration of the Holy Spirit's power. It is the demonstration that causes people to choose Jesus or not. Without demonstration it's a half of a gospel and another Jesus. The gospel Jesus preached was one of demonstration. The gospel entrusted to the apostles also was a gospel of of power and demonstration with an irrefutable witness that Jesus was truly risen from the dead.

"For the kingdom of God is not in word, but in power." (1 Corinthians 4:20)

These two verses are central to seeing the connection between the epistles of Paul and the Gospel of Jesus Christ. *Remember it was the preaching of the kingdom that gave birth to the church.* We are born again to see the kingdom and live from it, not just to go to church. The gospel is the power of God unto salvation. Power brings change. Jesus was the ultimate reformer. Most people hate change but Jesus loves it; he will even make heaven new, hence the new heaven and the new earth referenced in Revelation 21:1.

Jesus taught his disciples to live the kingdom, pray the kingdom and seek the kingdom. That wasn't enough; he also commanded them to preach the kingdom. He commanded them to preach the very same message he did. Jesus didn't tell people to do or preach things he wouldn't do or preach himself. He is our example because he always led by example. Unfortunately many of the leaders of today are trying to tell people to do things they have not done themselves; this hypocrisy and is a recipe for disaster. The blood of Jesus has made us kings and priests so preaching the kingdom should be as simple as describing our home or telling someone our address. Religion tries to complicate what grace has paid for and simplified through Christ Jesus. The message of the Kingdom is simple, Jesus is Lord and there is no other. Because Jesus is really Lord, it can be demonstrated in time and space through faith in him. We really have faith in him when we hear and obey him. As we hear and obey Jesus he manifests himself and the kingdom comes with power. Bill Johnson says this, "When we preach the kingdom, it creates an atmosphere conducive for the kingdom to come." That was a rough paraphrase, but you get the point. The message of his Kingdom makes room for the Lordship and supremacy of Christ to break into a human body or situation. Which is why the right message is important if we want the right results. The testimony of the Lord is sure when the word of the Lord is pure. If the message is diluted, it's usually because the one delivering it is living in compromise. In the kingdom of God, there is no compromise. In the kingdom, the vessel and the message must be pure. Our purity is God's number one priority in the kingdom. Ministering with power doesn't mean God is pleased. However, if a life is truly pure before the Lord it will be a life filled with power and character. Purity and power are necessary if we want to preach and demonstrate the kingdom of God authentically. The demonstration of the Spirit is not just the power gifts, but also the character of Christ in our daily lives. Remember friend if people don't see our integrity they will not want to hear our truth.

The Increase of His Government

The gospel is good news. The gospel of Jesus is the gospel of the kingdom because he is the king of the Kingdom. The good news is not just that we can go to heaven when we die, but at any time heaven could break in. When Jesus said, *"Repent, the kingdom of God is at hand,"* he was saying that the kingdom of God is within reach. He was saying that the time is now and the people are you. I echo some very similar words now, "Repent change the way you think. God is on your side because of Jesus' sacrifice; the kingdom could and will break in if you would only believe in Jesus." Jesus sent his disciples to preach and release the kingdom of God. In Matthew 9, Jesus told his disciples to pray that the Lord of the Harvest would send forth laborers into his harvest.

> *"But when he saw the multitudes, he was moved with compassion on them, because they fainted, and were scattered abroad, as sheep having no shepherd. Then saith he unto his disciples, The harvest truly is plenteous, but the laborers are few; Pray ye therefore the Lord of the harvest, that he will send forth laborers into his harvest."* (Matthew 9:36-38)

In Matthew 10, he was giving them power and sending them out. Matthew 10:1 says, *"And when he had called unto him his twelve disciples, he gave them power against unclean spirits, to cast them out, and to heal all manner of sickness and all manner of disease."* Before Jesus even gives them the message to preach he gives them power to demonstrate it. Bill Johnson said, "The gospel without power is not good news." I totally agree with him because Jesus never sent someone to preach without power. Jesus either gave them power or the people speaking were themselves the testimony of his power. Either way the gospel is the power of God that changes, heals, and eternally saves. The gospel that is preached also has the power to keep us. It was all made possible through Jesus' death, burial, resurrection, ascension and also his coming again at the end of the age. So Jesus gives the disciples power and then the message.

"And as ye go, preach, saying, The kingdom of heaven is at hand. Heal the sick, cleanse the lepers, raise the dead, cast out devils: freely ye have received, freely give." (Matthew 10:7-8)

The message Jesus commanded them to preach was the kingdom. Jesus doesn't say just be led; he commands them to do exactly what he knew the Father desired. This method is proclamation and demonstration. They are to announce or preach the kingdom and then to demonstrate it with supernatural power to restore life back to the way God intended it to be. Jesus didn't tell them to pray for the sick; he commanded them to heal the sick because he gave them power to do so. So it is with us. The same spirit that raised Christ from the dead lives in us and so we must heal the sick in Jesus' name. In the verses above go preach and heal are all in the active tense, meaning healing didn't stop when the apostles died or when the Bible was completed and printed. Honest Bible scholars who are true to the text clearly understand that the message of the kingdom and the power of the Holy Spirit are for today. I want to boldly tell you that the stripes on Jesus' back are not irrelevant or outdated. Healing still flows from those stripes and God's word is still true. The message of the kingdom makes room for the kingdom to come. The kingdom of God is not just healing; however, there is no sickness in the kingdom. So when the kingdom comes sickness leaves because the kingdom is dominant and where Jesus' dominion is sickness has to leave. It is then when people are forced to make a decision. Jesus' ministry gave people the option to make an educated decision about him because he manifested the kingdom. If we are his followers, we must also. Remember the message that Jesus tells us to preach is the message he backs up. The kingdom of God is not in word but in power. He backs his word up with power. That power flows from his love to the lost and dying so they can be translated out of the kingdom of darkness into the kingdom of his dear son Jesus.

In the gospel of Luke, there is a similar scripture, but there is a difference in the order or the method that is used to reach people. Luke 10:9 says, *"And heal the sick that are therein, and say unto them, The kingdom of God is come nigh unto you."* Here it is demonstration and explanation. In the previous verse it was *"preach the kingdom and heal the sick."* However in Luke it's, *"heal the sick and tell them the kingdom of God is come near unto you."* There is clearly a difference in method. The question is could there be a possible reason? My answer would be perhaps. Remember Matthew a Jew wrote the Gospel of Matthew to the Jews, while a Gentile named Luke wrote the Gospel of Luke. Luke was written to the Gentiles. When Jesus gave these instructions he was sending his disciples to the lost sheep of the house of Israel, see Matthew 10:6. However, demonstrating first and explaining later can more effectively reach the gentiles or unbelievers. We need less programs and more power, less talk and more action. Unfortunately many people know what we are going to say even before we say it. I personally believe we must demonstrate first and explain later, especially in nations where there is a church on every corner. Jesus has given us his power to demonstrate and his authority to explain. If the people haven't heard much about Jesus, telling them who he is and demonstrating his power is fine also. There is no set way to do things, which is why we need the Holy Spirit to teach us what to do in the moment. As humans we want a formula but God wants relationship.

The issue is not whether we preach first and heal second or heal first and preach second. The issue is they both must be done for the gospel to be the gospel Jesus and the apostles preached. For the gospel to be fully preached signs and wonders are a vibrant part of the real gospel. The gospel is good news. Good news to the sick is healing, good news to the lost is salvation, and good news to the poor is they get fed. The good news is a person. Jesus Christ of Nazareth is the good news. When he shows up the kingdom comes and what was impossible becomes possible. We have a lively hope because Jesus is the living God. Hope pulls the reality of faith into the now, and the kingdom manifests as we obey his word. Jesus' disciples had access to his power because they obeyed his word. He sent them out and as they obeyed, they naturally became supernatural. Jesus gave them power for a purpose, not just so they could have a revival meeting in a church building somewhere. We can pray for revival or become one; that choice will be determined by our obedience.

"Heal the sick, cleanse the lepers, raise the dead, cast out devils: freely ye have received, freely give." (Matthew 10:8)

Power is given freely but is only sustainable through wisdom. Wisdom causes us to obey Jesus and use his power the right way for the right reasons. Jesus is the wisdom and power of God and he always obeyed his Father. Power is to put Jesus on display not to draw people to us. Jesus revealed the Father by obeying him the same way we reveal who Jesus is as we obey him, which is the kingdom life in a nutshell. In a democracy, usually the popular vote wins; in the kingdom, what the King says goes. Often our relationship with God is defined by our democratic or Greek worldview. When I say that I am speaking to American Christians specifically. As I mentioned earlier, we must have a kingdom worldview if we are going to live for the King. Here is a brief Adam LiVecchi definition of a kingdom worldview. "We will do what God said in his word and is saying by his Holy Spirit at all costs no matter what because Jesus is Lord."

The kingdom is revealed and released through uncompromised devotion to the King and his word. In the kingdom of God, there is no fear or unbelief. Fear is just plain doubting God is who he says he is and that he will do what he said he would do. In life we will have to makes choices; these choices will either reveal who God is through our lives or continue to give the world a distorted picture of who Jesus is. When the kingdom of God breaks in, it is to point up to the king. When the kingdom breaks in, it is to soften the hearts and change the minds of people. God loved people enough to give Jesus; therefore, we must begin to love people enough to show them what Jesus is really like by our actions. The kingdom comes to change the way we think so we can change the way we live and the world we live in.

> *"But into whatsoever city ye enter, and they receive you not, go your ways out into the streets of the same, and say, Even the very dust of your city, which cleaveth on us, we do wipe off against you: notwithstanding be*

ye sure of this, that the kingdom of God is come nigh unto you. But I say unto you, that it shall be more tolerable in that day for Sodom, than for that city. Woe unto thee, Chorazin! woe unto thee, Bethsaida! for if **the mighty works had been done in Tyre and Sidon, which have been done in you, they had a great while ago repented,** *sitting in sackcloth and ashes. But it shall be more tolerable for Tyre and Sidon at the judgment, than for you." (Luke 10:10-14)*

My focus is on the bold words. When the kingdom comes, when signs and wonders follow or precedes the gospel proclamation, it should change the way people think. Repent means to change the way you think. It doesn't mean cry at an altar and never change the way you think or live. It means change the way you think and walk in the other direction. When we change the way we think, it is because we have allowed God to touch our hearts and change our minds. If we change our minds, we change our lives. Letting God touch our heart will change our mind and change our life. Here is a brief connection between the heart and the mind.

"For they considered not the miracle of the loaves: for their heart was hardened." (Mark 6:52)

The word considered means understand, comprehend or put together. Here the disciple's minds weren't working correctly because their hearts were still hardened. God's miraculous power and provision are supposed to soften our heart, change our mind, clear our vision, and correct our perception of reality and align it with God's word and purpose. Miracles can bring about citywide repentance and even nation wide transformation.

In the book of Daniel, there are two very clear pictures of how one miracle can deeply impact a nation and clearly reveal the superiority of God's Kingdom to any other kingdom. Nebuchadnezzar went to Jerusalem and besieged it. Therefore Jerusalem was under Babylonian captivity, which meant they were subject to Babylonian law and Israel was free slave labor to Babylon.

Eventually Nebuchadnezzar makes a law that anyone who doesn't worship the image of him will be thrown into a fiery furnace. Therefore three young men say no to idolatry. They were cast into the fiery furnace and then Jesus shows up. Shadrach, Meshach and Abed-Nego stood up for Jesus and he showed up for them.

"Many are the afflictions of the righteous: but the LORD delivereth him out of them all." (Psalm 34:19)

This verse is so visible in the book of Daniel. Their chains were broken, they were free and completely unharmed by the fire, and they didn't even smell like fire. Them not smelling like fire was also supernatural. I love this because it is prophetically pointing to Jesus who is the only one who can save us from hell's fire. Nebuchadnezzar was deeply moved when God showed up. Let's see the results of God showing up and delivering his people.

> *"Therefore I make a decree, That every people, nation, and language, which speak any thing amiss against the God of Shadrach, Meshach, and Abed–nego, shall be cut in pieces, and their houses shall be made a dunghill: because there is no other God that can deliver after this sort. Then the king promoted Shadrach, Meshach, and Abednego, in the province of Babylon. Nebuchadnezzar the king, unto all people, nations, and languages, that dwell in all the earth; Peace be multiplied unto you. I thought it good to show the signs and wonders that the high God hath wrought toward me. How great are his signs! and how mighty are his wonders! his kingdom is an everlasting kingdom, and his dominion is from generation to generation."* (Daniel 3:29- 4:3)

The king of Babylon understood that the Kingdom of God is everlasting simply because God broke into time and space. When divine intervention takes place, it reveals the everlasting kingdom of God and reveals his power to save from generation to generation. When Jesus shows up, a revelation of the kingdom comes to those who weren't even looking. Here king Nebuchadnezzar gets a

The Increase of His Government

revelation of a greater kingdom than his. It was the uncompromised devotion to God's law that caused Jesus to show up, which resulted in a wicked law being changed. Our faithfulness is what puts Jesus on display for others. The whole point of living a kingdom life now is that others may see Jesus. It is evident that Nebuchadnezzar had a change of heart and mind because he changed the law and told everyone in the world about a kingdom greater than his. The cities that Jesus did mighty works in did not repent but this one miracle caused a king to repent enough to change a law and tell everyone in the earth what God had done. That my friend is the good news of the Kingdom. Here is a prophetic picture of the gospel of the kingdom being preached in all the world in a moment of time.

As we continue on in the book of Daniel, we will see the kingdom breaking in again. Remember it's uncompromised devotion to God that causes the kingdom of God to break into our circumstances. God can sovereignly break in, but also we see all through the Bible that when people obey him he shows up and breaks in. The kingdom of God is released when God's word is not compromised. When we live the word, the kingdom comes. Knowing the truth isn't enough; we must live it out so others can see it and choose Jesus who is the truth. Daniel was one who lived the truth. He was of an excellent spirit according to Daniel 6:3. He was found faithful in all things. When the king needed a dream to be interpreted and no one could he could. In modern terms Daniel was the man! The princes and magicians of Babylon were jealous of his gifting and his position. They couldn't find anything wrong with him or his behavior, so they tricked the king and fabricated a law that would make Daniel guilty. The law was that for "thirty days no petition could be made to God or man except King Darius." So King Darius, a narcissistic egomaniac agreed and signed the law. Lawlessness is when the laws of man directly oppose the laws of God. It's kind of like calling a perverse relationship between two men a marriage. Well you get the point. So Daniel keeps praying and ends up paying. Daniel gets thrown into the lion's den.

"When a man's ways please the LORD, he maketh even his enemies to be at peace with him." (Proverbs 16:10)

Daniel's way of not compromising truly pleased the Lord. So much that a heathen king fasted all night for Daniel to live. The scripture says, *"If a man's ways please the Lord he will make even his enemies to be at peace with him."* Read Daniel 6:18-24 to get the full details of the story.

King Darius had a change of heart.

> Daniel 6:25-27 states, *"Then king Darius wrote unto all people, nations, and languages, that dwell in all the earth; Peace be multiplied unto you. I make a decree, That in every dominion of my kingdom men tremble and fear before the God of Daniel: for he is the living God, and steadfast for ever, and his kingdom that which shall not be destroyed, and his dominion shall be even unto the end. He delivereth and rescueth, and he worketh signs and wonders in heaven and in earth, who hath delivered Daniel from the power of the lions."*

When God protects his people, those who are not his people find out what God is really like. Now a heathen king is commanding the whole entire known word to tremble before the God of Daniel, not bad huh? Again King Darius receives a revelation of a kingdom greater than his. The king's repentance was seen in that he made a decree to all of the known world. Darius told the world the good news of God's kingdom. The testimony of the Lord is sure and in one moment because one man wouldn't compromise the whole world heard the good news of the Kingdom. It is through uncompromised devotion to God that the kingdom comes. The angel that shut the mouth of the lion came from the Kingdom of heaven to save Daniel on earth, so he could carry out heaven's plans. Look at what the scripture says about Daniel.

"Then was the king exceeding glad for him, and commanded that they should take Daniel up out of the den. So Daniel was taken up out of the den, and no manner of hurt was found upon him, because he believed in his God." (Daniel 6:23)

The testimony of what God has done should cause us to do what he is calling us to do. In the process of our obedience, we have access to his power and resources. Simultaneously, Jesus is conforming us to his image as we co-labor with him and he is forming himself in us as he speaks to us.

The Kingdom breaks in on a construction sight in New Jersey

I wanted to share with you a brief testimony of God's divine intervention in my life. It was a cold winter day on Friday, January 6, 2006. I was a plumber by trade. We were a non union shop working on a union sight. I know you are discerning conflict. Wow, you are pretty sharp. So as non-union plumbers we were always used to insulating our own pipes and weatherproofing our work. The union insulator who was about 6'1 and 245 pounds wasn't so excited that we were doing his job. Here is where the conflict begins. So my boss's son and this angry insulator are face to face. The pipe insulator could easily break this young kid's face. They are cursing at each other, and so it draws a small crowd of like 3-5 people, me being one of them. So I, empowered by the grace of God and the person of the Holy Spirit, humbly step in between the angry insulator and little mister wise mouth. I point at the angry insulator and say, "God shows mercy to the merciful." Immediately he closed his mouth turned around walked away and didn't say anything further. This was rather surprising. I was really happy not to have gotten beaten up. So after a few minutes I eventually went back to work not thinking much of what had just happened. The next day the man who was in charge of the plumbers for the company I worked for pulled me aside and said that the pipe insulator called our boss and left a message. This was the message he left, "When that kid preached to me, something closed my mouth, turned me around and walked me away, and I lost all control of myself." I was totally blown away. The man who told me this was not Christian but I was witnessing to him about Jesus. Mr. Angry insulator obviously was not a Christian, but he was testifying of a power greater than himself. I told the guy who was in charge who had relayed the message that my boss told him, that it was Jesus. What happened is God broke in with his kingdom and his dominion was manifested upon that man's mouth, body and feet. Jesus clearly and publicly exercised his dominion and had an unbeliever share the testimony. Jesus gave me courage to speak a peace making word. Remember the Holy Spirit is attracted to the word. The kingdom of God is manifested as we act on the word. When we do what we know to do, God reveals his power to those who don't know him.

CHAPTER 9

THE INCREASE OF HIS GOVERNMENT

Isaiah 9:6-7 says, *"For unto us a child is born, unto us a son is given: and the government shall be upon his shoulder: and his name shall be called Wonderful, Counselor, The mighty God, The everlasting Father, The Prince of Peace. Of the increase of his government and peace there shall be no end, upon the throne of David, and upon his kingdom, to order it, and to establish it with judgment and with justice from henceforth even forever. The zeal of the LORD of hosts will perform this."*

There is an eternity of depth in this small portion of scripture. In these two verses, a great mystery is revealed. The verses clearly reveal the God who put on flesh and gave himself for us. The child that was born was speaking of Jesus' humanity hence he often referred to himself as the "Son of man" modeling how man should live in perfect relationship to God. He also was the Son of God, meaning he was God in the flesh. He was fully man so he had to sleep; he was fully God so he could sleep in a storm. He was fully man so it was possible for him to die; he was fully God. No man could take his life; he himself willingly laid it down with the power to take it up again on the third day. While Jesus was offering himself on the tree no man took his life; he offered it up to his Father. Even while he hung there naked and blood was pouring out of him, his kingdom was still increasing; his government was still increasing with no chances of it ever ceasing. Literally while blood was leaving his body, his kingdom was marching forward, his purposes cannot be stopped. While Jesus was dead for three days in a tomb, his government was still increasing. There is no stopping him! Radical Islam can't stop him, a lukewarm church cannot stop him, and global government ruled by an antichrist spirit cannot stop him. He is Christ the Lord, and his kingdom is marching forward. I believe you want to move with him so we are going to look to his word to be a lamp unto our feet and a light unto our path so we can move forward with his kingdom that knows no end. His written word is the logos or lamp and his now word, which would be his rhema word, which is the light. The rhema word proceeds from him the logos word. John 1:1 says, *"In the beginning was the Word, and the Word was with God, and the Word was God."* The Greek word used for Word in this verse is referring to the Lord Jesus Christ.

To properly understand the kingdom of God we must be careful and diligent to understand his word. If we are going to partner with Jesus in his prophecy that states, "of the increase of his government and peace there shall be no end," we must learn how to according to his word and not our opinion. The body of Christ must learn to know God and partner with him on his terms, in his timing, according to his eternal purposes that are in Christ Jesus from before the foundation of the world. So his government increases many different ways and we are going to touch on some of them to help us "see the hope of his calling." It's important to know the hope of his calling because it's our calling because we are called to be in him.

> *"That the God of our Lord Jesus Christ, the Father of glory, may give unto you the spirit of wisdom and revelation in the knowledge of him: The eyes of your understanding being enlightened; that ye may know what is the hope of his calling, and what the riches of*

The Increase of His Government

the glory of his inheritance in the saints." (Ephesians 1:17-18)

Our calling is his calling. Meaning we are called to know him and do as he did. 1 Corinthians 1:9 says, *"God is faithful, by whom ye were called unto the fellowship of his Son Jesus Christ our Lord."* As we get to know Jesus, his kingdom or government increases in our life. In Isaiah 9:6-7, the revelation of who Jesus is precedes the prophecy of what he will do. As we get to know him, he naturally does what he said he would do as we hear and obey him. Also, in the Lord's Prayer both in the beginning and at the end is a revelation of the Father. As we focus on God, he will do his part; our part is to focus on and fellowship with his Son Jesus. Simultaneously we naturally get to know him and discover our purpose and the form of expression that we are to communicate Jesus to a lost and dying world. Some would say I am not called to evangelism and I would say then you are not called to fellowship with him. Jesus himself said in Matthew 12:30, *"He that is not with me is against me; and he that gathereth not with me scattereth abroad."* The kingdom or government increases as we get to know Jesus and properly represent him to those who don't know him but desperately need him. Usually when we say we are not called to something it's because fear is holding us back from serving the Lord wholeheartedly. Remember friends there is no fear in the kingdom of God.

The government increases as the King speaks. Often times when we hear God speak we forget that it is a king who is speaking and only obedience is acceptable and pleasing to him. God does not speak from a democratic seat; he speaks from a sovereign and eternal throne meaning what he says goes. So as God speaks and reveals himself to us, his kingdom increases. God loves therefore he speaks because what he says is what changes us. As we change things around us change and his kingdom comes. His kingdom can come because his throne has wheels. (See Ezekiel 1:13-17) The first time we see the Holy Spirit in the Bible he is moving upon the face of the waters. When the Holy Spirit is moving, the Kingdom is coming. Just for your information the Holy Spirit is "kingdom now." Jesus really is Lord now even though we don't see everything directly under his leadership just yet, but it's coming even the anti-Christ can't stop him. In spite of the global government that is forming, Jesus' government is still increasing. One day every eye will see that Christ alone is supreme. One day every knee will bow and every tongue will confess that Jesus Christ is Lord.

> *Behold, he cometh with clouds; and every eye shall see him, and they also which pierced him: and all kindreds of the earth shall wail because of him. Even so, Amen. I am Alpha and Omega, the beginning and the ending, saith the Lord, which is, and which was, and which is to come, the Almighty.* (Revelation 1:7-8)

Jesus will show everyone at one time who he is and it cannot and will not be stopped. Jesus has been given a name above all names; therefore, every knee will bow to him. They will bow to him because he is the king of Kings. Every tongue will confess because he has been given the name above all names. When you think Kingdom just think Jesus, when you think of his government increasing just think of him revealing himself. He never changes but that doesn't mean there is not more. It means the opposite; because he never changes there is always more of him to be revealed to us his children.

Partnering with the King

Jesus taught his disciples to pray "thy kingdom come" because of several reasons. They are as follows:
• Jesus only said what he heard the Father say.
• It's the Father's good pleasure to give us the Kingdom.
• The Holy Spirit loves to move.
• Because of the prophecy his Spirit inspired Isaiah to speak and write, *"Of the increase of his government and peace there will be no end."* (John 12:49, Luke 12:32, Genesis 1:1, Isaiah 9:6-7)

Jesus peacefully crushes Satan under our feet and his government extends when humanity makes peace with him through receiving his sacrifice on Calvary. Through the blood of Jesus alone we have peace with God. When Jesus tells us to pray for something, it's because he intends to give us what he has told us to ask for in prayer. This principle is also seen in Psalm 2:8 and connects to Matthew 28: 18-20; it is also clearly seen in Matthew 9:37-38, 10:1-8. God uses prayer and prophecy partnering together to bring about a manifestation of promise, through the obedience of our faith. This is the will of God. Faith is the currency of the kingdom, but love is the economy of the kingdom, while hope is the outlook on the market's future. God's kingdom always comes through his love that can't be measured by anything but the cross. His kingdom always comes through the wisdom of his power. To be a part of kingdom advancement we must be fully confident in Jesus' leadership. The more confident we are in his wise leadership the easier it becomes to partner with him. We are co-laborers and co-heirs with Christ; therefore, partnership is easy as long as we are Christ centered and not self-centered. Heaven is Christ centered hence *"On earth as it is in heaven"* see, Revelation 5:6.

The visible manifestations of the kingdom increase as we obey Christ's teachings. Jesus instructed his disciples about how to live in Matthew 5-7, so his Lordship must be lived out practically and not just believed doctrinally. In Matthew 6, Jesus teaches his disciples and us how to pray. We also learn one of the languages of the kingdom, which is forgiveness. Remember there is no un-forgiveness in the kingdom. We only get in the Kingdom because Jesus is willing to forgive us. God is good and he loves and forgives. Jesus loved enough to preach, teach, heal and die. Jesus did therefore we must. We are sent to preach and heal in his name because he preached and healed.

> *"And he entered into a ship, and passed over, and came into his own city. And, behold, they brought to him a man sick of the palsy, lying on a bed: and Jesus seeing their faith said unto the sick of the palsy; Son, be of good cheer; thy sins be forgiven thee. And, behold,*

> *certain of the scribes said within themselves, This man blasphemeth. And Jesus knowing their thoughts said, Wherefore think ye evil in your hearts? For whether is easier, to say, Thy sins be forgiven thee; or to say, Arise, and walk? But that ye may know that the Son of man hath power on earth to forgive sins, (then saith he to the sick of the palsy,) Arise, take up thy bed, and go unto thine house. And he arose, and departed to his house. But when the multitudes saw it, they marvelled, and glorified God, which had given such power unto men. And as Jesus passed forth from thence, he saw a man, named Matthew, sitting at the receipt of custom: and he saith unto him, Follow me. And he arose, and followed him."* (Matthew 9: 1-9)

This is a radical story of God's kindness that leads men to repentance. Here Jesus explains what healing illustrates. Sin to the soul is like sickness to the body. Healing is an illustration of forgiveness. Forgiveness brings about reconciliation, meaning because God is good we are reinstated to a right relationship completely on his merit. Jesus heals the lame man illustrating he has the power or authority on earth to forgive sins. Here Jesus demonstrates his eternal spiritual authority by healing someone's temporal lameness.

Jesus continues on his journey and then calls Matthew the tax collector. Directly after Jesus healed a lame man saying that he had the power to forgive sin. Jesus befriended Matthew the tax collector. Which is a radical story of love and forgiveness. Matthew was a Jewish man but he worked for Rome. Rome was taxing and oppressing Israel at the time. Matthew made his living by adding more money to the taxes of already overtaxed people. He was a professional extortionist and he extorted his own people. It's clear that he wasn't very popular among his own people, which is a perfect reason for Jesus to choose him. Truly "not many might men are chosen." When Jesus said, "follow me" to Matthew he was saying you are forgiven. One of the ways the kingdom advances is through forgiveness. Forgiveness is very simple but often we struggle with it. This is not necessary. We must put our faith in Christ when he prayed, "Father forgive them, for they know not what they do." Matthew used to be a Publican or a tax collector. He used to rob God's covenant people, but after he was forgiven and followed Jesus he was used to give people the most valuable writing ever, the Gospel of the Kingdom. A good majority of the rest of the "kingdomology" in this chapter is from a man who was a professional crook before he met Jesus. (I made that "kingdomology" word up.) Jesus came along and made room for Matthew and as Matthew got to know Jesus he changed. As we are transformed from faith to faith and glory to glory the kingdom increases As we mature in Christ, his kingdom increases in and through us as we walk with and obey him.

The kingdom comes through preaching and healing. What Jesus did was so effective that he has decided that we should do it also. Jesus preached, taught and healed and that is the work of the ministry we are all called to that is referenced in Ephesians 4:11-13. This is how the kingdom comes. We are sent so that the kingdom will come. God never sends us without power. Bill Johnson, Senior Pastor of Bethel Church in Redding California says, "The gospel without power is simply not good news." All through Matthew 9 Jesus is healing people. Then in Matthew 10, he gives his disciples authority to do what he had just taught them. True spiritual authority is to equip and release people, not control and manipulate them. If you go to a church and the Pastor is the only one who prays for people run for your life.

"And as ye go, preach, saying, The kingdom of heaven is at hand. Heal the sick, cleanse the lepers, raise the dead, cast out devils: freely ye have received, freely give." (Matthew 10:7-8)

When the kingdom is preached, the king shows up and healing occurs. Jesus taught his disciples to preach a message that created an atmosphere for miracles.

"And heal the sick that are therein, and say unto them, The kingdom of God is come nigh unto you." (Luke 10:9)

Here when the sick are healed, the kingdom has come nigh or near to them. The kingdom of God affects the body. The body of Christ is seeing an increase of the kingdom and one of the ways it is manifesting is in healing. This is similar to the book of Acts.

And by the hands of the apostles were many signs and wonders wrought among the people; (and they were all with one accord in Solomon's porch. (Acts 5:12)

> Watch the government increase. Acts 5:14-16 says, *"And believers were the more added to the Lord, multitudes both of men and women.) Insomuch that they brought forth the sick into the streets, and laid them on beds and couches, that at the least the shadow of Peter passing by might overshadow some of them. There came also a multitude out of the cities round about unto Jerusalem, bringing sick folks, and them which were vexed with unclean spirits: and they were healed every one."* If our hands don't heal people our shadows never will. Here the kingdom increases from the hands of a man to his shadow. Peter's shadow had the power to heal because he was walking in the light. Again we see how the kingdom or government increases as people obey God. When we are faithful with little we will be given much. If you are praying for people with knee pain and back pain just keep being faithful because in no time people may just be getting out of wheel chairs or having their vision or hearing restored."

Remember in Matthew 10:8 it also says "cast out devils." Deliverance is not a spiritual gift per say however it could fit under the category of a healing or a miracle as listed in 1 Corinthians 12 by Paul the Apostle. Deliverance is an eviction notice to the devil. When evil spirits are cast out of people, it bears witness to satan that he will be thrown off this planet and into the lake of fire forever one day. I am not sure he likes that.

"But if I with the finger of God cast out devils, no doubt the kingdom of God is come upon you." (Luke 11:20)

The kingdom is increasing again. Deliverance evicts the devil. When healings occur, the kingdom comes "near," when deliverance takes place the kingdom comes "upon." Being near someone is very different than being upon someone. The good news of the Kingdom gets even better. The kingdom is not limited to heaven, or the healing of a sick body or even the eviction of an evil spirit. The kingdom of God comes to live on the inside of us when Jesus truly becomes the one and only Lord of our life.

"Neither shall they say, Lo here! or, lo there! for, behold, the kingdom of God is within you." (Luke 17:21)

Often we look for something outward but Jesus reminds us of what he has put on the inside of us. The outward life cannot determine true success, but if the inward life is successful, the outward life will reflect the success that comes when you allow Jesus to rule you from within. I want you to understand success as Jesus understood it. Success can be defined simply by living a life that is pleasing to the Father. We are seated with Christ in heavenly places so we live from heaven toward earth. Christ and his kingdom live on the inside of us so he can live his life through us as we die to sin and self and are led by his Holy Spirit. That is good news and you are absolutely a vibrant part of God's redemptive plan.

Jesus doesn't have to change himself but he loves to change people and anything that isn't expressing his love and wisdom. If someone or something doesn't express his love and wisdom in truth and sincerity, he desires to change it. We enter into this labor as he speaks to us and we obey him. The kingdom is the manifested reign of the King's love and wisdom. Jesus' passion to reform and change is unsurpassed by anyone ever. Jesus put on flesh to redeem and reform humanity. We are born again not just to go to heaven but also to be a part of heaven coming to earth. Most of the church wants to just go to heaven, but Jesus wants heaven to come to earth. We must renew our minds and start to live from Jesus' perspective and not from our own fears or disappointments or biblical misunderstandings. When Jesus died and rose again, a reformation began. The increase of his government is the manifestation of this reformation that will bring all things under his rule; his realm is coming from heaven to earth. His reign is forever, and we are his royalty partnering with him. This is the mystery of his will and you and I are privileged to be a part of it all. (The word reformation is found once in the Bible see Hebrews 9:8-12 to see its context.)

Reformation is needed if revival is going to be sustainable. Jesus should not have to keep raising the church from the dead if it's seated with him in heavenly places. In reality we don't need a revival because nothing in the Kingdom is dead. What we need is an alignment. This issue is not that the church is not seated with Christ in heavenly places; the issue is that it doesn't believe it really is. The mind of Christ allows us to be seated with Christ in heavenly place and live from heaven toward earth. We need to align our perspective with the truth of God's word and kingdom and then our experience will change. Often people want their expricen to change before their perspective changes, but in reality we need to change our perspective if we expect to see things really change. The only safe place for the church is in the kingdom. Jesus doesn't just wake up dead churches, or heal broken hearts or sick bodies. All of that is a part of what he loves to do but in the famous words of Randy Clark, "There is more!" The Apostle Paul wrote about Jesus having complete preeminence. The Gospel of Matthew tells us that all authority belongs to Jesus. I just want our vision of him to grow. Jesus came in the likeness of men, and he was touched with our infirmities and also tempted and yet remained sinless. It's great that he can fully relate to our struggle. However, all too often we relate to Jesus more as him being a man and forget he was God in the flesh. I just want to put you and even myself in remembrance that he is an everlasting King who works all things after the counsel of his own will. We must continue to learn and remember who Jesus truly is. The kingdom of God provides a safe environment for us to get to know our King. The kingdom is a safe haven for broken people who are hungry for Jesus.

The Increase of His Government

The good news gets better.

> Colossians 1:18-20 says, *"And he is the head of the body, the church: who is the beginning, the firstborn from the dead; that in all things he might have the preeminence. For it pleased the Father that in him should all fullness dwell; And, having made peace through the blood of his cross, by him to reconcile all things unto himself; by him, I say, whether they be things in earth, or things in heaven."*

This was written about 60 years after the death of Christ. About 35 years later on the Greek Island of Patmos, John received the revelation of Jesus Christ. In that revelation, we see the prophecy of Isaiah 9:6-7 coming into manifestation.

"And the seventh angel sounded; and there were great voices in heaven, saying, The kingdoms of this world are become the kingdoms of our Lord, and of his Christ; and he shall reign for ever and ever." (Revelation 11:15)

Christ's preeminence over all things will be manifested when the seventh angel sounds his trumpet. Are you ready? The good news gets even better as the kingdom comes. As great as this verse is, it's simply not enough to Jesus; he wants more.

Jesus will not just change the earth; he will change heaven as well.

> Revelation 21:1-6 states, *"And I saw a new heaven and a new earth: for the first heaven and the first earth were passed away; and there was no more sea. And I John saw the holy city, new Jerusalem, coming down from God out of heaven, prepared as a bride adorned for her husband. And I heard a great voice out of heaven saying, Behold, the tabernacle of God is with men, and he will dwell with them, and they shall be his people, and God himself shall be with them, and be their God. And God shall wipe away all tears from their eyes; and*

there shall be no more death, neither sorrow, nor crying, neither shall there be any more pain: for the former things are passed away. And he that sat upon the throne said, Behold, I make all things new. And he said unto me, Write: for these words are true and faithful. And he said unto me, It is done. I am Alpha and Omega, the beginning and the end. I will give unto him that is athirst of the fountain of the water of life freely."

Even after this his government will continue to increase as God reveals his kindness that is toward us in Christ Jesus, see Ephesians 2:6-7. Remember the words of Randy Clark, "There is more!"

CHAPTER 10

THE GREAT COMMANDMENT AND THE GREAT COMMISSION.

The church doesn't have a Kingdom; the Kingdom has a church. So it is with the Great Commandment, which fuels the Great Commission. Even in the Scriptures the Great Commandment to love God and man is given before the Great Commission. My spiritual Father Steve Stewart of Impact Nations says it like this, "The church doesn't have a mission; the mission has a church." (Mark 12:29-31, Mark 16:15-18) The Great Commission is not love; it's an expression of love. As I started to discover all that God was doing in the earth, I expressed my deep desire to be a part of it. Jesus said to me, *"Adam you are because you are a part of my body and everything I am doing you are attached to because you are in me and this is a mystery."* That brought a deep rest to my soul because I truly desired to be a part of what God is doing. Deep inside if we are all honest we truly want to be a part of what God is doing. In his word he tells us how. The word tells us and his Holy Spirit leads us in the when and where of his will that is part of the *"mystery of his will."* This is a pretty good deal. Now that we know that God is subduing all things under the feet of his dear Son Jesus, we get to play our part in it. We cannot do God's part, and he will not do ours. What is amazing about God's will is that we are not separate from it, but rather it fully involves us being in relationship with him which leads us to a life of obedience empowered by grace. This is the only life that we were all truly created for.

"He that hath my commandments, and keepeth them, he it is that loveth me: and he that loveth me shall be loved of my Father, and I will love him, and will manifest myself to him." (John 14:21)

As we obey him, he manifests himself and his Kingdom comes. We don't obey God to prove to him we love him, but rather we obey him because we love him simply because he first loved us.

Love is the most empowering attribute of who God is. God's first commandment to us is for us to love him.

> Mark 12:29-31 says, *"And Jesus answered him, The first of all the commandments is, Hear, O Israel; The Lord our God is one Lord: And thou shalt love the Lord thy God with all thy heart, and with all thy soul, and with all thy mind, and with all thy strength: this is the first commandment. And the second is like, namely this, Thou shalt love thy neighbor as thyself. There is none other commandment greater than these."*

His first priority is that we would love him. Hearing him empowers us to love him. Before there is a command to love, there is a command to listen; love listens. His voice strengthens us to keep his word. His love for us empowers us to love him and others. The same way when he speaks a word it has the power to perform it. Another similar reality is when Jesus commands us to do something, he gives us the power to do it and that my friend is good news. Jesus tells us to do the impossible; he is always involved in the impossible if we are obeying him. Jesus commands us to do the impossible. He commands us to do things that we could only do through him, he does this so we would never try it without out him. We are called to the work of faith with power; we are called to the labor of love. In loving Jesus, we obey him and begin to love our neighbor as our self. If we love him, we will obey his word.

If we love our neighbor we will hear Jesus' commission to teach people to observe all things he has commanded. Before we teach the world to obey Jesus, we must learn ourselves. Kingdom order is that first we do then we teach, but western culture is often we teach things we don't do ourselves. A small example of this is you can go to college and get a business degree from a teacher who never owned a business a day in his life. Leadership in the kingdom is not so, first we do then we teach others to do as we have we have done or we are hypocrites. Paul said it like this *"follow me as I follow Christ."* Righteous living should always precede a following or it will be the blind leading the blind. We have charismatic people in the body of Christ leading people into a ditch. We need to live right and lead by example and not by concept, gifting, teaching or a charismatic personality. God is calling forth those who love him enough to obey him to lead his people. Kingdom leadership looks like Christ Jesus; he is our example. I have no interest in a man's anointing or mantle; I only have an interested in Jesus' anointing and mantle. When Christ is our first love we don't exalt man; we exalt Him alone. In the kingdom of God, he alone is exalted.

We only love Christ as much as we love people. 1 John 3:17 says, *"But whoso hath this world's good, and seeth his brother have need, and shutteth up his bowels of compassion from him, how dwelleth the love of God in him?"* Remember the love of God is for people not just for goose bumps at a church service or prayer meting. Loving our neighbor usually gets worked out into very simple and plain circumstances. If you would like to see some examples check these scriptures out: Luke 10:33, Luke 16:19-31, and Matthew 25: 35-46. There is a unique connection between Jesus and the poor; we will touch on that later. We must learn to love our neighbor even if our neighbor is gay, or is a terrorist, or a drug dealer. We love them by being kind enough to show them Jesus in our actions, preach Jesus with our words and demonstrate his power when needed. It's time we learn to love like Jesus. It's not enough to believe the truth and speak it, but we must learn to love enough to live it out. The word becomes flesh in us when we obey Jesus. Our relationships are a great measure of if we have learned to love or not. Love doesn't burn bridges; love forgives even when someone doesn't say they are sorry. Forgiveness is one of the greatest expressions of love. Forgiveness is love on the defense while acts of compassion is love on the offensive. We love as much as we are willing to forgive those who haven't said they are sorry. Loving our neighbor is not just doing good to people; it is also choosing to forgive, pray and bless others who may not feel the same way about you. If we are not a forgiving people, we will not stand under real persecution. When we choose to forgive, we choose love. Remember there is no unforgiveness in the kingdom of God. These are some very simple and basic expressions of love. The Great Commandments empower us to live out the Great Commission. The Great Commission is the Gospel of the Kingdom.

The Gospel of the Kingdom must be defined. There are all different teachings on this. I would like to propose a very simple definition of the "Gospel of the Kingdom." Matthew and Mark both contain different elements of the Great Commission. We look at both to see the big picture.

> *"And Jesus came and spake unto them, saying, All power is given unto me in heaven and in earth. Go ye therefore, and teach all nations, baptizing them in the name of the Father, and of the Son, and of the Holy Ghost: Teaching them to observe all things whatsoever I have commanded you: and, lo, I am with you alway, even unto the end of the world. Amen."* (Matthew 28:18-20)

All authority has been given to Jesus and he tells us to go to all people and teach them all things he has commanded. That is the Gospel of the Kingdom. Heaven comes to earth when we do what Jesus has commanded. This clearly teaches us how to partner with Jesus. These verses paint the big picture in a very clear way. The big picture is everyone and everything coming completely under the authority of Christ Jesus who is already highly exalted above all. We partner with the Father through the Holy Spirit and he brings this about as we obey him. As the church obeys Jesus, "the bride makes herself ready." The only way we make ourselves ready is by obeying King Jesus in carrying out what he has commanded and commissioned us to do in his name.

> *"And he said unto them, Go ye into all the world, and preach the gospel to every creature. He that believeth and is baptized shall be saved; but he that believeth not shall be damned. And these signs shall follow them that believe; In my name shall they cast out devils; they shall speak with new tongues; They shall take up serpents; and if they drink any deadly thing, it shall not hurt them; they shall lay hands on the sick, and they shall recover."* (Mark 16:15-18)

These verses are the little pieces that put the big picture together. We are all commanded to go and preach. You may say I am not called but that is only fear and or unbelief. Jesus says you are called and chosen, and he even ordained you in John 15:16 which says, *"Ye have not chosen me, but I have chosen you, and ordained you, that ye should go and bring forth fruit, and that your fruit should remain: that whatsoever ye shall ask of the Father in my name, he may give it you."* If we want to bring forth fruit we must go and preach. The seed that produces fruit is the word, and to bring forth fruit we must go into all the world.

Often times people from cultures where idolatry is preeminent understand the importance and prophetic significance of water baptism. I was in India once where I witnessed people healed, saved, baptized and renamed in a matter of three hours. They were immediately baptized and completely disassociated from their past. There were buried in baptism and risen with Christ. These beautiful people had their names changed from false Hindu god names to normal Christian names. These people came up out of that dirty water smiling ear to ear. This was an awesome experience because we didn't have to spend five weeks convincing these people to be baptized; they just knew immediately that it was necessary because they had just made Jesus their Lord. Another time in Haiti at a medical clinic, my friend Barbara was in line praying for the sick when suddenly a young woman began to manifest demons. So they eventually got my friend Mac and I and we commanded all the demons to leave in Jesus name and after some time they all left her. The very first question the woman asked was, "When can I get baptized?" We never once mentioned baptism. She just knew in her Spirit that it was necessary because she had just been delivered from the devil and wanted to immediately disassociate herself from darkness completely and immediately. This totally blew our minds. We just laughed and said, "Wow Jesus that was really cool!"

Speaking with other tongues is very important in advancing the Kingdom. Having a prayer language or speaking in tongues is very important when it comes to increasing in faith.

"But ye, beloved, building up yourselves on your most holy faith, praying in the Holy Ghost, Keep yourselves in the love of God, looking for the mercy of our Lord Jesus Christ unto eternal life." (Jude 1:20-21)

When our faith is built up, it keeps us in love. Faith works through love and faith keeps us in love. When we speak in tongues according to Paul the Apostle, we speak "mysteries to God." Jesus said, "To you it has been given to know the mysteries of the Kingdom." If we sow mysteries to God, we will reap mysteries from God. (1 Corinthians 14:2, Matthew 13:11) Tongues also are other natural languages when we go to other people groups. God had sovereignly given people a language they have never learned before instantly so they could preach Jesus to those who need him. We see this clearly in Acts 2.

Mark 16:18 says, *"if they can drink any deadly thing, it shall not hurt them."* Here God is speaking about divine protection. Where the gospel goes, signs and wonders go as well as persecution. However, divine intervention or protection also comes with the gospel. God promises to protect us, but he also promises persecution, which is part of the Gospel. Unoffended believing believers must embrace both aspects of these truths. Jesus also said that those who believe will lay hands on the sick and they shall recover. He didn't say only the Pastor or elders will lay hands on the sick. He said, "If you believe they shall recover." (A rough paraphrase putting the emphasis on his point.) Remember friends there is no fear, doubt or unbelief in the Kingdom of God. Jesus didn't ask us to pray for the sick if we felt led or called. He commanded us to in Matthew 10:7-8 which says, *"And as ye go, preach, saying, The kingdom of heaven is at hand. Heal the sick, cleanse the lepers, raise the dead, cast out devils: freely ye have received, freely give."* When the message of the Kingdom is preached there then comes the demonstration of its power for "the Kingdom of God is not in word but in power." We have access to power as we believe God's word and act on it. There are several things that stop us from acting on it and they are fear, doubt, unbelief and false teaching. Unbelief is simply a belief without a corresponding action that manifests your belief. Preaching the Gospel and healing the sick are commands not options or callings. As a church, we need to return to our first love and first works and come back into agreement with the purposes of the kingdom. God works from the top down at times, but Jesus worked from the bottom up. Culture is shaped from the top down, while movements start from the bottom up. If we are going to see an explosion in the middle we will need both. Jesus came from heaven and lived toward earth to re-form the culture of the earth from earth to heaven, which is why he taught his disciples to pray, "on earth as it is in heaven." Jesus spent a lot of time ministering to the sick and the poor. He also spent time with the rich and influential; however, he spent most of his time with the poor. If we are going to be those who partner with the kingdom, it will certainly take us among the poor, the sick and the disenfranchised. There is no poverty or sickness in heaven; therefore, it must be kicked off the planet. There is no abortion in heaven; there is no sexual perversion or exploitation in heaven. There are no lost people in heaven; therefore, we must preach the gospel to all of creation so they can find the only truth— the Lord Jesus Christ. All of the social issues such as poverty, abortion, and the sex-trade are not social or political issues they are gospel issues. When the gospel of the Kingdom is preached injustices are addressed and people are liberated.

CHAPTER 11

BLESSED ARE THE POOR

Luke 6:20 says, *"And he lifted up his eyes on his disciples, and said, Blessed be ye poor: for yours is the kingdom of God."* Jesus blesses the poor in Spirit and the economically poor. Someone who is poor in Spirit could possibly be rich. Zacchaeus of Luke 19: 1-10 was wealthy and was poor in Spirit as soon as Jesus showed up. He then without Jesus even asking him gave to the poor. When salvation came to his house immediately a portion of his money went to the poor, which is very interesting. My Spiritual Father and friend Steve Stewart says this, "The Spirit of the Lord is upon me because he has anointed me to preach the gospel to the middle class." He's obviously joking. The anointing to preach the gospel has a specific audience and that is the poor. The gospel can and must be preached elsewhere and everywhere; however, Jesus was anointed to preach to the poor. If Jesus did we must. If we are in him, we are called to preach to the poor and serve them just as he did. As we serve them, we are really serving him. We don't have to feel called; we simply are. Whether we like it or not the poor in the earth and in our community know how much faith we really have. The poor are rich in faith, and the riches of God's grace are often manifested amongst the poor. An authentic gospel can be discerned several ways one of them being, is it preached to the poor? All through the scriptures, Jesus has a very unique relationship with the poor. The King is very fond of the poor; therefore, the kingdom must serve the poor because it belongs to them. Globally, the middle class is shrinking and the gap between the rich and poor is growing quickly; therefore, we must care for the poor if we are truly Kingdom minded. The governments of this world are not anointed to preach to or care for the poor. The church is and we can draw from the resources of the Kingdom to do so. To whom much is given much is required. It doesn't say to whom much is given much is suggested, it says to whom much is given much is required. We are blessed to be a blessing not only to be the fattest people group on the planet. North American Christians are the fattest people on the planet. I am one of them and we need to repent. I am not trying to make anyone feel guilty. I am simply saying that we waste more food in one day than about 1 billion people on planet earth eat a day. This is an unspeakable injustice, which has brought me to tears many times. Often tears are the first step to change. Remember, Godly sorrow works repentance. Repentance is part of Kingdom life. Repentance is not confessing sins; confessing sins is confession. Repentance is God revealing what we do not know so we can change the way we think and see. When we change the way we think we change the way we see and then we can follow him and live out his dream for our life. Sustainable change happens when we change together and keep one another accountable.

Understanding God's heart for the poor and oppressed is essential to living a Kingdom life. A good majority of the ministry of Jesus was among the poor. If Jesus being God in the flesh was focused on the poor then for us not to be is ignorant. The poor are so rich in faith they don't have to understand something to believe it; they just believe. If you want to go to the best seminary in the world go to Haiti, Mozambique, or Nicaragua and observe the poor for six months or a year. I can honestly say I have learned more working with the poor than at any conference or seminar. I often find myself crying because my head doesn't understand what my heart is learning. If learning doesn't make us tender towards the poor and the oppressed then we certainly aren't learning to love.

An unforgettable lesson of Desperation in Carrefour, Haiti

It was September 2009. My dear friend Rev. Mac Barnes was preaching at an open-air meeting in Carrefour, Haiti. There was at the very least 2,000 people there. God had given me some words of knowledge about four conditions that he wanted to heal that night. So Mac turned to me by the Spirit of God knowing that I had some words of knowledge. So I called them out and immediately a crowd of well over 100 people rushed forward to be prayed for. I came down off the stage to lay hands on the sick. There were four security guards standing within seven feet of me keeping the crowd back from me. The Bible talks about how the crowd pressed in to touch Jesus and this was happening to me. It was unforgettable, see Mark 5:24 Luke 5:1, Luke 8:42. They weren't coming to be prayed for by a famous evangelist. I was completely unknown to them; it was even my first time in Haiti. They were so desperate to be prayed for they were fighting in line! It was awesome to see such faith and hunger in motion. They were pushing because they were desperate to be healed and they didn't have much doubt that they weren't going to be healed. That night tumors disappeared and almost everyone was healed. There were so many healings that we had to stop the testimonies because the sound crew had to break down the speakers for church the next morning, and it was getting late. It was great to see people being healed and saved almost effortlessly. The Kingdom of God truly came to Carrefour Haiti that night it was absolutely amazing. I was so grateful to God that the Gospel was preached and people were healed, but the people's hunger is what affected me the most. When I look back on that night I then begin to understand a little bit more clearly as to why Jesus said, *"Blessed are the poor for theirs is the Kingdom."*

I will share a few other encounters I had with Jesus in the face of the poor, I hope they bless your heart to be tender and open your eyes to the person in front of you. As I began to follow God's call on my life, it took me all over the world. He put a love in my heart for the poor. In February 2008 while I was with Impact Nations in **India,** God spoke to me in a profound way. I was at a medical clinic in south India. It was hot, humid and pouring rain. I was standing in line with an elderly man. I was being friendly with him so I gave him a hug as an action of love because I could not speak his language. When I hugged him, immediately Jesus spoke to me. He said, *"I was sick and you came to me."* When I heard this I began to weep like a baby, Jesus had just spoken to me from the least of these. He said whatever you do unto the least of these you do to me, and so he spoke from the person he identifies himself with.

"For I as hungered, and ye gave me meat: I was thirsty, and ye gave me drink: I was a stranger, and ye took me in: Naked, and ye clothed me: I was sick, and ye visited me: I was in prison, and ye came unto me." (Matthew 25:35-36)

I knew this was Jesus speaking to me because he said, *"I was sick and you came to me."* This rocked my world. After that I lost ability to function for a while. This had such a traumatic effect on my soul. For the rest of the day I worked in the medical clinic totally messed up and full of joy unspeakable.

  As the journey continued in September of 2009, I was in **Montevideo, Uruguay**. In the beginning of the trip my friend Teofilo Hayashi and I prayed for a woman with a tumor, and it instantly disappeared. Later on this same trip we were walking to church on Sunday morning. I saw a street boy who looked hungry so I invited him in to have coffee and breakfast with me. It was he and I sitting at the table. As he was sitting there with me eating, I was telling him that Jesus loved him in Spanish. I stopped and said to the Lord, "He really smells Lord." Immediately Jesus responded to me, *"What, Adam, you do not like the way I smell? I was hungry and you gave me food."* Here again Jesus was speaking in the face of the least of these. As I am sitting with this young man who is way too young to be homeless, I am weeping because of what Jesus just said. This really blew me away. The boy comes with us to church and sits in the front row with my friend Teofilo and I. Later in the service he gets saved. I felt like I got saved all over again when the Lord spoke to me about the boy's smell as his smell. As I sat by the homeless I learned more about the fragrance of Christ than in any church service. This experience had a profound effect on my heart because I cannot forget the stench of that boy that was really the fragrance of Christ in the face of the least of these.

About a month later, in **New Jersey** in October of 2009 I organized my first annual Prophetic Conference called "Awake to Righteousness." I had some food prepared in the back for the speakers. As service was over and the speakers and I went back to eat some amazing Cuban sandwiches, I noticed there were several people back there that were not invited. Usually I have no problem being strong with people but that time I did not for some reason. Several "down and outers" were back there eating with the speakers. So later that night, "I said, Lord, do these people just not respect my authority because I am young? Is that why they were back there?" Jesus said, "No, you prayed to be like me and these are the kind of people I attract." Well out come the tears and confession and repentance all over again. Now Jesus is speaking on behalf of the down and outers. Religious hierarchies and boundaries mean nothing to King Jesus. Quite frankly he would probably rather eat with the "down and outers" than the conference speakers or Bishop Nobody. We must learn to calibrate our hearts to hear what Jesus is saying even if it goes beyond our religious thinking of how something should be.

Carrefour, Haiti on January 12 2010. This earthquake shook Haiti, and brought a nation to its knees in thirty seconds. I happened to be there during the quake. I was in the epicenter of the quake, and God miraculously spared my life. I was able to come out and return home in February of 2010. The Lord allowed me to experience what he said in his word.

"Whose voice then shook the earth: but now he hath promised, saying, Yet once more I shake not the earth only, but also heaven." (Hebrews 12:26)

I love this scripture; it has become flesh in me because I lived through this experience of God's voice, which truly shakes the earth. That same voice called my name twice and scared the hell out of me.

When I came back from Haiti the second time, I stayed in the **Bavaro, Dominican Republic** for a few days to relax and also to preach. One day I was walking back from the Internet café. As I was walking back to the church, I saw a Haitian in the garbage eating. So I grunted at him and signaled for him to get out of the trash and so he did. I walked over to him and gave him enough money for a decent meal because he was obviously hungry. His shirt was shredded and so I took my tank top off and gave it to him. As I walked away discouraged about this poor man's condition I took my golf shirt out of my book bag and put it on. Then suddenly the Lord spoke to me and said, "That is how you feel about me, you gave me the cheaper shirt and you kept the nice one for yourself." So I asked Jesus to forgive me for giving him the cheaper shirt. Jesus needed to be clothed in the face of the needy but I was more concerned about me. When Jesus speaks to you, it will cause you to see yourself, people and life for what it really is. This messed me up and showed me I am messed up. I was honored that he would even say something like this to me. He trusted that I would know it was he, and not try to bind the devil when it was actually Jesus speaking. The sharpness of Jesus' word cut into my heart and made me aware of its hardness. Then he was able to come in, touch it, heal it and make it tender to his voice. It is a good thing when the Lord brings correction into our life. It may not feel good but the long-term results are worth a little temporary pain, and besides Jesus gave us the comforter to help us through the rough times.

Carrefour, Haiti on August 8, 2010. It was a humid night and I was doing an open-air crusade in not the nicest of neighborhoods. There was roughly 1800 people there. It began to pour and pour as I was preaching so I got off the stage and told the people that since they were wet I was going to get wet and pray for anyone and everyone who needed prayer. So a huge crowd of people came forward for prayer. So the prayer team went down to pray for the sick and demonized. People were getting healed and demons were being cast out. One thousand people stayed in the rain to dance and praise Jesus; it was beyond words. I had joy unspeakable. After I had finished praying for the people who were in line, I began to dance and sing and scream Jesus. Then a few moments later, I stopped and looked into the crowd. When I focused on the crowd, I began to choke up and tear. It was then when Jesus spoke to me and said, "This is why I said blessed are the poor for theirs is the kingdom." I fell apart and started crying and dancing and thanking Jesus for speaking and allowing me to be around people who love him so very much. The poor and Jesus are inseparable according to the Scriptures. King Solomon knew this even before Jesus taught Matthew 25 to his disciples.

"He that hath pity upon the poor lendeth unto the LORD; and that which he hath given will he pay him again." (Proverbs 19:17)

If you want to give something acceptable to someone who has everything give to those who have nothing.

> *"In Acts chapter 10, Cornelius of the Italian band was a devout man who feared God. The two things he did that showed he feared God was prayed and gave alms to the people or money to the poor. Him praying and giving was before the revelation of Jesus came to his household through the ministry of the Apostle Peter. Let's see what his praying and giving on earth did in heaven. And when he looked on him, he was afraid, and said, What is it, Lord? And he said unto him, Thy prayers and thine alms are come up for a memorial before God."* (Acts 10:4)

The substance of his faith manifested as a memorial before God. What we do on earth clearly affects eternity. Giving to those who are down and out gets the attention of the high and lofty one, God almighty. This is profound, yet it teaches us about the Kingdom. We humble ourselves to be exalted; we serve God and he recognizes us, but in the world the people who are served are the ones who are recognized. Everything is different in the Kingdom. We will get more into this later.

Cornelius' praying and giving manifested as a memorial before God. Let's learn about Jesus as a King who rules from his throne at his Father's right hand. There are several things that will make Jesus get up from his throne. When Jesus returns to the earth to rule with an iron rod, he will get up off his throne. There are two others I would like to mention.

> "But he, being full of the Holy Ghost, looked up steadfastly into heaven, and saw the glory of God, and Jesus standing on the right hand of God, And said, Behold, I see the heavens opened, and the Son of man standing on the right hand of God. Then they cried out with a loud voice, and stopped their ears, and ran upon him with one accord, And cast him out of the city, and stoned him: and the witnesses laid down their clothes at a young man's feet, whose name was Saul. And they stoned Stephen, calling upon God, and saying, Lord Jesus, receive my spirit. And he kneeled down, and cried with a loud voice, Lord, lay not this sin to their charge. And when he had said this, he fell asleep." (Acts 7:55-60)

Here Jesus is standing at the right hand of the Father as Stephen is getting stoned. The persecution of his church causes Jesus to arise from his throne. The church that will stand up for Jesus causes the king in his kingdom to stand up and observe what is going on. The second thing that causes the King to arise from his throne is found in Psalms 12:5, which states, *"For the oppression of the poor, for the sighing of the needy, now will I arise, saith the LORD; I will set him in safety from him that puffeth at him."* God gets off his throne for the poor! Remember the enemy of the poor is the enemy of the Lord. Truly there is nobody like Jesus. The poor and the persecuted make Jesus stand up off his throne. Jesus honors the poor and the persecuted and so we must also. There is something so pure about a believer who has been persecuted for righteousness' sake. It's almost like the more they are persecuted the more Jesus' light shines upon and through them.

The Increase of His Government

Another life changing day in the Kingdom of God occurred on April 1st 2009. I had just arrived in **Sao Paulo, Brazil.** My friend Teofilo picked me up from the airport and told me we were going to see the Heavenly Man tonight. Immediately I knew he was supposed to lay hands on me and pray for me. God gave us favor that night and we sat in the front row. After he was done preaching, we wanted to receive a prayer of impartation, but he just went into the back room of the church to eat. So Teofilo and I not taking no for an answer snuck backstage where a really cool usher took us right into meet Brother Yun or the Heavenly Man. Brother Yun was in federal prison in Beijing, China for the Gospel of Jesus Christ. He had two broken legs thanks to the communist party of China. However, the Angel of the Lord opened the prison door for him just like he did for the Apostle Peter in Acts 12 and he walked out a free man. Yes with two broken legs he walked out a free man! So as I am standing before him, there is a businessman talking to him while playing with his Blackberry. I was really disturbed by that man's outright rudeness. Anyway while I am standing there the Lord said to me, *"Adam you are standing before me right now."* I said what Lord? He said, *"Adam that man is fully dead."* It was no longer brother Yun living but Christ living in him. It was just Jesus with no additives! When he hugged me, it was like Jesus hugging me. This man bore on his body the marks of Jesus Christ. He was counted worthy to suffer for the Kingdom. That night he laid hands on Tefilo and I and prophesied to us and we were at loss for words for about an hour at least. When he laid hands on us, the Kingdom came with power, and it had the fragrance of Christ on it. I share this with you to get you hungry for Jesus and the kingdom. The poor and the persecuted both understand risk. If you are going to be someone whom Jesus stands for and honors, you must be willing to take risks. What if we would have gotten thrown out of the church that day and looked like idiots? Remember what we learned from the poor and the persecuted. God responds to desperation!

If we check out world history, nations who oppress the church and the poor usually fall apart within a hundred or two hundred years. In Egypt's case it was four hundred years, you get the point. With that being said, God was going to judge Babylon and Daniel gave a word to Nebuchadnezzar concerning the poor.

> *"Wherefore, O king, let my counsel be acceptable unto thee, and break off thy sins by righteousness, and thine iniquities by showing mercy to the poor; if it may be a lengthening of thy tranquility."* (Daniel 4:27)

America's tranquility has been lengthened because it takes care of the poor. If we stopped doing that, only God knows what would happen on this soil. The poor are not a political or a religious issue; they are a Kingdom issue that cannot be ignored any longer. When we ignore the poor, we are really ignoring Jesus.

> *"Then shall the King say unto them on his right hand, Come, ye blessed of my Father, inherit the kingdom prepared for you from the foundation of the world: For I was an hungred, and ye gave me meat: I was thirsty, and ye gave me drink: I was a stranger, and ye took me in: Naked, and ye clothed me: I was sick, and ye visited me: I was in prison, and ye came unto me. Then shall the righteous answer him, saying, Lord, when saw we thee an hungred, and fed thee? or thirsty, and gave thee drink? When saw we thee a stranger, andtook thee in? or naked, and clothed thee? Or when saw we thee sick, or in prison, and came unto thee? And the King shall answer and say unto them, Verily I say unto you, Inasmuch as ye have done it unto one of the least of these my brethren, ye have done it unto me."*
> (Matthew 25:34-40)

This is the king speaking; therefore, this is a Kingdom issue not to be taken lightly. Here Jesus the Savior is speaking about eternal judgment; we might want to pay attention.

CHAPTER 12

THE THRONE OF GOD

Jesus sits at the right hand of the Father in heaven. This is very interesting because Jesus is to the right of the Father but also in the center of everything else, see Hebrews 1:3, and Revelation 4:5, 5:6. Heaven is obviously a little different from earth; however, Jesus is perfectly suitable to rule both. Jesus rules and reigns from his throne, but he never changes. Everything in heaven is alive; therefore, everything is named. I will go into this in detail in another chapter but for now let's stay on the throne because everything is measured by the throne. Jesus is literally at the right hand of the Father yet is in the center of heaven in the center of his throne? The reason that Jesus is to the right of the Father yet the center of all things is that the Father only relates to humanity through Jesus therefore everything is measured by him. He is the standard; he is the beginning and the ending it is all about him.

> *"Therefore thus saith the Lord GOD, Behold, I lay in Zion for a foundation a stone, a tried stone, a precious corner stone, a sure foundation: he that believeth shall not make haste. Judgment also will I lay to the line, and righteousness to the plummet: and the hail shall sweep away the refuge of lies, and the waters shall overflow the hiding place."* (Isaiah 28:16-17)

Jesus is that precious cornerstone and his plumb line is righteousness and justice. Righteousness and justice are also the foundation of the throne. The strength of Jesus' dominion is his everlasting righteousness and his justice to and for all. Jesus cannot be a respecter of persons because he cannot change. The throne is great but it's really about who is sitting on it. The worship in the throne room is amazing but the worship still is not equal to the King on this throne that is why the worship never stops.

"Let us therefore come boldly unto the throne of grace, that we may obtain mercy, and find grace to help in time of need." (Hebrews 4:16)

We should know about what we are told to boldly approach. Here we learn the throne has a name and its *"grace"*, hence the throne of grace. Jesus boldly gave himself for us and so we can boldly come to him because he has made a way for us. Jesus is not just the only way; he is our way. Remember he is the grace of God and we can only come to the Father through him. One thing to learn about grace is it is specifically for the *"time of need."* Grace is released in the time of need. A brief example is when Stephen is being stoned in Acts 7 and he sees Jesus standing at the right hand of God. The grace he needed was to see Jesus standing and he did. Remember Jesus stands for those who stand for him. That gave Stephen the courage to get through what he was going through. We are told to boldly approach the throne because there is room for us in the Kingdom. Jesus has not only made a way for us, but he has also prepared a place for us.

"Let not your heart be troubled: ye believe in God, believe also in me. In my Father's house are many mansions: if it were not so, I would have told you. I go to prepare a place for you." (John 14:1-2)

Jesus was telling his disciples to simply not be afraid or dismayed because he was preparing a place for them. He is saying there is room in the Father's house for them. Beloved there is room for you in the kingdom of God. You may have been hurt or rejected by religion, but the Father loves and accepts you; he has room for you. Jesus prepared a place for you and the Holy Spirit is sanctifying you and leading you to exactly what Jesus has framed out just for you. Grace is unmerited favor, which makes room for those who could not make a way for themselves. We are to boldly approach the throne so we can come and worship Jesus and hear what he has to say. Remember friends it's far more important what Jesus has to say to us than what we want to say to him. When we abide in him in love his voice is our first priority. Before we speak he knows, but before he speaks we do not know. As we approach the throne boldly, it must be in the posture of humility, and one of humility's greatest qualities is it listens. The thrones of man are about controlling, but the throne of God is about man being liberated by God, so we can fully love God and people just like Jesus did.

Psalm 89:14 says, *"Righteousness and Justice are the foundation of your throne; Mercy and Truth go before your face."* The foundations of something are what hold the structure up. The foundation of a building is the most important thing. Jesus himself mentioned that the house that endured the storm was the house that was built on a rock, and that rock was him. We build on Jesus when we do what he is has commanded in his word and is saying by his Holy Spirit. The real issue of the throne is that Jesus is Lord. The question we have to ask ourselves is if he is really the Lord of our life? Do we do what he says? The throne is grace, the seat is mercy and righteousness and justice are the foundations. These virtues are very useful if we are trying to discern whether or not God's authority is backing something up or if we are doing something in the flesh. If justice, righteousness, mercy and grace are present then most likely our decision is honorable to Jesus. As we approach the throne of Grace, we are to obtain mercy because we are going to need it for ourselves, and we are also going to need some extra mercy to give away to others. Mercy picks us up when we fall and grace causes us to stand. Righteousness is our relationship with God through Christ and Justice deals with how we relate to others. God requires from us what we can only get from him.

"He hath showed thee, O man, what is good; and what doth the LORD require of thee, but to do justly, and to love mercy, and to walk humbly with thy God?" (Micah 6:8)

This verse clearly shows us what the King expects from us. He expects us to walk and live like Jesus. The way we truly walk humbly with our God is by doing justly and loving mercy. We should deeply love mercy because we get it and don't deserve it. Mercy is us not getting the judgment we deserve and grace is God giving us what we do not deserve and cannot earn. Often in Christianity we compare ourselves and our actions to people, but in all reality we should compare everything to God's Word and his throne. Remember Kings speak from their throne. They judge and rule from their throne. The good news is that God is on his throne; it gets even better. We are called to be "seated with Christ in heavenly places." This is so we live from divine perspective, have access to his resources and have his authority to carry out his will in the earth, hence *"thy will be done thy kingdom come on earth as it is in heaven."* (Ephesians 2:6, Matthew 28:18-20)

The throne of God is the place where there is no greater or higher authority. The real Supreme Court is in the heavens where Jesus is seated at the right hand of the Father. The United States Supreme Court has people put their right hand on the Bible to assure the court that they will tell the truth. This act is deeply profound and it points directly at God's sovereignty. The reason they tell people to put their right hand on the Bible and swear to tell the truth is simply because the Bible is the truth! Also the United States recognizes a higher authority than even the Supreme Court. We should continue to pray for America that they would continue to recognize the God of heaven as Supreme and return to him. The United States government is patterned after the book of Deuteronomy. Representative government was God's idea. We should continue to pray for our elected officials to make decisions that are in favor of God's word. Remember "the heart of the King is in the hand of the Lord and he moves it where he pleases." I want to encourage you when lawlessness begins to run rampant and it is already in some measure, to remember that God is still on his throne, and he sits in the heavens and laughs; so don't let the enemy steal your joy. Remember the Joy of the Lord is our strength and if the enemy can steal our joy then we will not be able to stand in the evil day. My challenge to you is that you continue to pray for godly men and women to get into key spheres of influence like Joseph, Daniel and Esther did in the days of old.

Jesus taught us to pray *"thy kingdom come"* and it can and will. The kingdom can come because the throne has wheels. Jesus had a mobile ministry; he was and is always on the move. In Ezekiel 1, the throne of God was pursuing Ezekiel and he ended up face down worshipping. The throne is a place where God is to be worshipped. When the throne of God breaks into an atmosphere, it produces worship. The fruit of heaven invading earth is true worship. Jesus' authority caused people to bow down and worship him. When spiritual authority is used properly, it causes people to worship God not exalt man. Spiritual authority is not to draw people to us, but rather to cause others to worship Jesus in Spirit and in Truth. When the Kingdom of God is descending upon a specific geographic location you will see large gatherings of different tribes and tongues coming together to worship Jesus. I call this one of the tokens from the throne, see Revelation 5:9. The throne is not only a place from which God speaks and rules; it's also a place of worship. We don't just approach the throne to worship God, but he comes and inhabits the praises of his people. He is not only waiting for us to approach him, but as we worship he comes and enthrones our praise. God deeply longs to be with us. The kingdom of God is a perfect environment for fellowship with God. Remember we were created to know and fellowship with God. He created us so he could love us and in turn we could love him back. Mike Bickle of the International House of Prayer in Kansas City says it like this, "God is looking for voluntary lovers."

As we boldly and diligently pursue the ascended Christ, his presence continually descends upon us and we carry with us his fragrance as we go. Boldness comes upon us as we seek after Jesus, see Acts 4:13. We boldly approach the throne of grace because Jesus boldly came to the earth to die in our place. We love him because he first loved us, and we seek him because he came to seek and to save us. There are two things a Christian must be absolutely familiar with. They are as follows: the cross and the throne. Apostolic Christianity tends to focus a lot on the Cross,

Adam LiVecchi

and Prophetic Christianity tends to focus a lot on the throne of God. What's great is Christ is at the center of both, being the eternally slain lamb who is seated on the throne even now.

CHAPTER 13

ALLEGIANCE. ALLIANCE. CITIZENSHIP

Understanding allegiance, alliance and citizenship is key if we are going to be so heavenly minded so that we will be some earthly good. Often we hear people say something like this, "You are so heavenly minded you are earthly good." They may not be directly saying it to you or me but it is something that we in the church world have heard for quite some time. Unfortunately, it's just not true because to really affect the earth with the leaven of the Kingdom, we must have the mind of Christ, which is pretty heavenly minded. Jesus said all authority was given to him and so he sends us to teach people to obey all things he has commanded. Our first and only allegiance must be to Jesus Christ. All authority has been given to him because he is the King of Kings and the Lord of Lords. Because Jesus possesses all authority all of our allegiance is to the Lamb that was slain.

"Which in his times he shall show, who is the blessed and only Potentate, the King of kings, and Lord of lords; Who only hath immortality, dwelling in the light which no man can approach unto; whom no man

hath seen, nor can see: to whom be honor and power everlasting. Amen." (1 Timothy 6:15-16)

Jesus dwells in light unapproachable, gives unspeakable joy, and his riches are unsearchable. He is and does exceeding abundantly more according to the Spirit. He offered up his Spirit from the cross and gave to us his church. The more and more revelation we have of Jesus the more our allegiance to him is strengthened. It's the Father's good pleasure to give us the kingdom and he gives it to us by revealing Jesus. The kingdom comes as Jesus is revealed which is why when Jesus showed up he said, "Repent the kingdom of God is at hand." On the day of his revealing, the kingdom showed up and marched forward with every step Jesus took on the earth. Jesus told people to repent or change they way they thought because he knew it was the Fathers good pleasure to give people the Kingdom. Knowing the Fathers heart makes ministry simple and gives us confidence. Remember there are no insecure people in the Kingdom of God.

Here is another reference in the scripture that further reveals the reality that when Jesus shows up the kingdom comes.

> Matthew 16:15-19 says, *"He saith unto them, But whom say ye that I am? And Simon Peter answered and said, Thou art the Christ, the Son of the living God. And Jesus answered and said unto him, Blessed art thou, Simon Bar–jona: for flesh and blood hath not revealed it unto thee, but my Father which is in heaven. And I say also unto thee, That thou art Peter, and upon this rock I will build my church; and the gates of hell shall not prevail against it. And I will give unto thee the keys of the kingdom of heaven: and whatsoever thou shalt bind on earth shall be bound in heaven: and whatsoever thou shalt loose on earth shall be loosed in heaven."*

In the verse above Jesus immediately identifies the source of Peter's revelation. I want to purpose to you that Jesus knew where Peter's revelation came from because he knew where his revelation came from, see John 5:20. Immediately as the revelation of Jesus' true identity came from the Father Peter was given the keys of the Kingdom. True revelations from God lead to a responsibility from him, and we will need his authority to accomplish his purposes. This process according to Jesus gives the Father pleasure. It's his good pleasure to give us the Kingdom, and it's our privilege to partner with Jesus. The good news is not just that when we die we go to heaven because Jesus died and rose again. The good news is experienced every day as heaven comes to earth through our obedience to God. I am not diminishing not going to hell and exalting some kind of false utopia on earth. I am merely putting our attention toward Christ and his kingdom in the here and now. Our allegiance has a lot to do with our alliances. If our allegiance is compromised often our alliances are off also. It goes the opposite way as well. If we have unhealthy relationships or alliances then our allegiance can also be affected. Relationships in the body of Christ usually suffer more damage than relationships in the world. When I was unsaved I had two friends that fought with fists and within twenty-five minutes they were back in the same car being driven home by yours-truly. Yet there are many Christians who hold bitterness with one another for years and have no interest in resolving conflicts biblically and peaceably. The deeper issue is not our alliances in this case but our allegiance. If we are fully committed to obeying Jesus then we will do the very best we can to straighten out our issues with one another as fellow citizens from above.

In the obedience of faith is where we will find our most valuable relationships or alliances. If someone doesn't desire to be faithful to Jesus, they will not be faithful to you. In a true apostolic community, it must have a prophetic culture if is going to be sustainable. An apostolic community doesn't gather merely over ideas and theories but they gather over Jesus and the advancement of the kingdom through the preaching of the Gospel and the obedience of the faith that Paul made reference to in Roman 16:26. This doesn't mean we tolerate false doctrine because there are no false doctrines in the Kingdom. However, gathering over beliefs is not enough. It must be backed up by consistent actions that are congruent with those beliefs or we are hypocrites. A faith that cannot be demonstrated is no faith at all because faith without works is dead, and there is nothing dead in the Kingdom of God. Our allegiance is to the foundation and chief cornerstone.

> "For through him we both have access by one Spirit unto the Father. Now therefore ye are no more strangers and foreigners, but fellowcitizens with the saints, and of the household of God; And are built upon the foundation of the apostles and prophets, Jesus Christ himself being the chief corner stone; In whom all the building fitly framed together groweth unto an holy temple in the Lord: In whom ye also are builded together for an habitation of God through the Spirit." (Ephesians 2:18-22)

The fist alliance of the church is the two ministries that are built directly upon Christ himself. These are foundational ministries that are necessary for a healthy community of people to move forward in the foreordained purposes of God. The reason being is that Prophets prophesy or foretell what God is doing and Apostles carry an authority to move forward and have people follow them in the labor of the Gospel.

There is much more to it but keeping it simple our allegiances and alliances must be solid if we are going to be a part of Nebuchadnezzar's vision that Daniel interpreted where he saw a rock destroying the other kingdoms, see Daniel 2:34-44. The book of Daniel is a very powerful book. It is full of divine intervention and Kingdom principles that are true regardless of time, culture or social and economic differences. The power of God and the revelation of the Kingdom of God in the book of Daniel touch three powerful truths that are the title to this chapter. Daniel, Shadrach, Meshach and Abednego were citizens of Israel, and they were taken captive into Babylon. These four young men were citizens of another land that had different laws that were not to be compromised. Here their allegiance to the Lord their God was unshakable even at the threat of death itself. Truly they were part of a Kingdom that did not shake. Their allegiance with God was the strength of their alliance with one another. May this be true about our lives. Their oneness of heart caused God to show up on their behalf. They were committed to obedience whether by life or by death. When people are that faithful to God, they will be loyal to others around them. Their citizenship meant different laws, and a different allegiance and different alliances. They were not after personal gain, or a compromise induced promotion. Uncompromised devotion to God is what manifests his Kingdom in the earth. To keep the concept of allegiance simple God loves us, and we love him by obeying him. He speaks and we obey. The four young men in the book of Daniel had Jesus as their common denominator; their life was built upon what he said. Their allegiance, alliance and citizenship all had to do with how they lived their life, and so it should be with us.

Relationships in the Kingdom of God are more than a lifetime; they are eternal. The more and more we walk with Jesus the more we will value each other and authentic relationships. A Kingdom relationship is simply two people or more coming together for the purposes of God. It's Jesus and authentic faith that leads to action for his honor that keeps Kingdom relationships together for a lifetime. Unfortunately, half of the church can't even stay married to one person of the opposite sex for a lifetime, let alone have lifelong meaningful and fruitful relationships. Our alliances say a lot about us. Remember there were five wise virgins and five foolish virgins. There were not three foolish virgins and two wise virgins together. We deeply must consider those we yoke ourselves to. When compromise seeps into the heart of a believer one of the first things that changes is their associations or alliances. When the wrong things influence people, then they will probably be associated with the wrong people. I personally have seen this to be true on several different levels. I have seen pastors be influenced by people that they have given their ear to but the results were less than favorable. I have seen young people be influenced by their past and return to it. I have seen people have relationships with the wrong people and watched their life fall apart. Whether we want to acknowledge it or not influences and alliances also shape our life. Here are the benefits of being influenced by the right kind of person or people.

> "*Blessed is the man that walketh not in the counsel of the ungodly, nor standeth in the way of sinners, nor sitteth in the seat of the scornful. But his delight is in the law of the LORD; and in his law doth he meditate day and night. And he shall be like a tree planted by the rivers of water, that bringeth forth his fruit in his season; his leaf also shall not wither; and whatsoever he doeth shall prosper.*" (Psalm 1:1-3)

Those who do not take wrong counsel get right counsel from the absolute of God's word, and they prosper in what God has called them to do. Psalms and Proverbs are filled with knowledge about how to select our friends and alliances. A real friend will tell you what you need to hear not what you want to hear. It's actually what we don't want to hear that makes us what we are called to be. Often people run from the most valuable relationships God has designed for their life when they are told something they don't want to hear. Here is a valuable key to understand about Kingdom relationships.

"*Iron sharpeneth iron; so a man sharpeneth the countenance of his friend.*" (Proverbs 27:17)

Iron sharpens iron, but never without friction. It's actually the friction of the iron striking the iron that sharpens the sword. Often what we avoid is what we really need. Valuable relationships and ministry alliances will never be without friction. Usually if someone has a bad alliance in their life it's because their priorities are wrong. In God's economy we will never have to sacrifice our allegiance for our alliances. Another way to say it would be, we don't have to please man to have favor with man. If our ways please the Lord, he will even make our enemies be at peace with us.

"*When a man's ways please the LORD, he maketh even his enemies to be at peace with him*". (Proverbs 16:7)

This was true for Daniel because a heathen King fasted and prayed for him all night so he would not be eaten by lions, see Daniel 6:17-22. Pleasing God is a much better choice. One of the sole purposes of our alliances is to assist one another in pleasing God through the obedience of faith. True alliances are the fruit of our allegiance to Jesus. So as we set our hearts to obey Jesus and walk forward with him we then will naturally find people around us that we are aligned with. Our alliances are as important as the tracks of a train.

Kingdom Alliances
This is what a God ordained friend would do for you.

1. Pick you up if you fall (Matthew 14:31)
2. Defend you when you are not there (1 John 2:1)
3. Rebuke you when you are wrong (Mark 8:33)
4. Push you if you become complacent (The mind of Christ)
5. Cause you to become accountable when you become successful (The mind of Christ)
6. Tell you when you need a break (The mind of Christ)
7. Challenge you to step out in faith (The mind of Christ)
8. Love you at all times (Proverbs 17:17)
9. Will celebrate you and not just tolerate you (a common church phrase)
10. Provoke you to good works (Hebrews 10:24)

These are only a few. God will certainly add to what is here. I encourage you to wait on the Lord for a few minutes and see what he will say to you. Get your journal or a piece a paper and let the mighty Holy Spirit speak to you. Write down what he says to you.

Have you ever meet someone and said, "Where do I know you from?" Then they reply, "I don't know you really look familiar." Then as the conversation continues you realize you don't know them by the flesh but by the Spirit. Meaning you guys are both citizens from above and when you said they looked familiar you we merely moving in the gift of discerning of Spirits as Paul mentions in 1 Corinthians 12:10. You just happened to discern their citizenship.

Philippians 3:20-21: *"For our citizenship is in heaven, from which we also eagerly wait for the Savior, the Lord Jesus Christ, who will transform our lowly body that it may be conformed to His glorious body, according to the working by which He is able even to subdue all things to Himself."*

Directly attached to our citizenship is the hope and promise that Jesus will subdue or put everything under him. If this doesn't cause us to live differently I don't know what will. Our citizenship determines our allegiance and our alliances. God's authority gives us identity and identity has a lot to do with who we are, who we associate with and how we behave. I will give you a brief example that is drastic so what I am saying becomes a little clearer. Suppose we see the President of the United States eating out of a trashcan. Because of who he is, we would obviously think that is strange due to the fact that he is the chief of the White House and can go almost anywhere to eat for free. Here the President's identity shows us there is a serious issue with the President's behavior. Often this is how we look in the Spirit as citizens from above when we take part in sin. Unfortunately, we live with less than Jesus has provided. It's time to learn that we are citizens from above who are seated with Christ in heavenly places and to start acting like God's children instead of orphans or bastards. When God reveals to a believer who they are in Christ that lawless spirit of a bastard son is broken off. When God reveals that we are truly accepted and he calls us his beloved, the orphan spirit of rejection gets broken off. It is then when God begins to entrust us with inheritance. Not knowing who we truly are simply means we really don't know who Jesus is. When Jesus rebuked the seven churches in Asia in the Book of Revelation there were many problems, which can be simplified. The churches had an issue in their allegiance, and in their alliances. One church had lost their first love and another church tolerated Jezebel. Due to their allegiance being corrupted and their alliances being tolerant of evil through compromise they were not behaving like citizens from above do. So Jesus comes with a rebuke to line the church back up with the Kingdom. This happens when Jesus speaks and we listen enough to obey.

CHAPTER 14

ADOPTION, SONSHIP, INHERITANCE, KINGS AND PRIESTS

In the Kingdom of God, there is a process to that which God is doing. We can learn this Biblically by what he has done. We also continue to learn this experientially as we walk with God. The Kingdom of God is not like a microwave oven; it's more like a slow cooker. A simple word of faith teaching would go something like this: seed, time and harvest. The most painful of the three is the time factor. However, our maturity process does have to do with time.

"But let patience have her perfect work, that ye may be perfect and entire, wanting nothing." (James 1:4)

The work of patience is one of perfection or maturity. We mature over time. This is seen first in the natural world where natural time has a lot to do with physical growth. However, spiritual maturity has less to do with time and more to do with obedience. We mature through obedience, or become deformed through disobedience. A deformed Christian is simply one who conforms to the ways or the principles of this world. As Kingdom people, we are called to be transformed therefore we are reformers by nature. As citizens from above, it's only natural that we change the world. When the world in us has been changed then the world around us is bound to change. Everything is changing but Jesus, which is part of the good news of the Kingdom. What's amazing is as we walk with God we change but he doesn't have to.

Maturing and changing are very different. Jesus was fully God and fully man. As a man who was born from a woman, he had to mature in the natural process of life. Jesus was also fully God and so he could not change who he was. He was God from before the foundation of the world. He has always been the slain lamb, the creator and sustainer of all things. With that being said I want to place our attention on the maturing of his humanity, with his unchanging divinity as the foundation so as not to ever reduce Jesus to just being a normal man. Beloved normal men are not born from a virgin. I guess you get the point; Jesus is God in the flesh. Listen to the wisdom of the wise men.

"Saying, Where is he that is born King of the Jews? For we have seen his star in the east, and are come to worship him." (Matthew 2:2)

These men knew he was born King; it wasn't something he would inherit. It wasn't that man would appoint him or that he would even have to fight for his position. It's just who he was. These men are coming to worship a baby about two years old. They knew who he was, and so they responded the only right way by worshipping him. Soon after Christ was born Joseph and Mary left for Egypt and escaped Herod's genocide of Hebrew children. Jesus as a child was a political refugee. However, he's not just a political refugee, but he is our refuge and an ever-present help in time of need. Joseph then had a dream that it was safe to leave and so he left according to the revelation he was given. Years later Joseph and Mary went to Jerusalem to keep the Passover. They left and Jesus stayed in Jerusalem. When they came back for him Mary asked him, "Why have you done this to us?" Here is Jesus' response.

"And he said unto them, How is it that ye sought me? wist ye not that I must be about my Father's business?" (Luke 2:49)

Here we see that Jesus was about his Father's business. They didn't understand what he was saying but he did. He obviously wasn't referring to Joseph because he was a carpenter and Jesus was in the temple expounding on the word of God to the religious leaders. The Father's business is to reveal Jesus see, Matthew 3:17, 16:16-17, 17:1-5. Jesus was always about his Father's business. At this age, he was thought to be roughly about twelve years of age. So for another eighteen years he lived in obscurity, until the Father revealed him at John the Baptizer's church service in the wilderness. John the Baptizer had to baptize Jesus because John was a Levite and according to the law Levites had to consecrate the Lamb for Passover. This prophetic act was why Jesus said to John, *"Come it is now time for us to fulfill all righteousness."* See Matthew 3:15-17. Jesus didn't say that because he needed John to be righteous, but because the law demands the priesthood to consecrate the Lamb and that's what the baptism was about. Jesus was identifying with our sinful condition but he himself was sinless. As a matter of fact he was John's righteousness also. It is there roughly eighteen years later where God affirms what Jesus already knew as a boy. It was now time for Jesus to go into his ministry. Here we see the revealing of identity is necessary for ministry, hence "This is my beloved Son in who I am well pleased." Later as Jesus was getting ready to ransom his life for many he said something very profound. It showed Jesus' human maturity process spiritually the same way he went from Mary's womb to being a boy in the temple to being a grown man in the river Jordan.

John 14:9 says, *"Jesus saith unto him, Have I been so long time with you, and yet hast thou not known me, Philip? He that hath seen me hath seen the Father; and how sayest thou then, Show us the Father?"* Jesus went from being about his Father's business, to being publicly affirmed by his Father, to saying that "if you have seen me, you have seen the Father." From this scripture, the writer of Hebrews finds authority to say this in chapter 1 verse 3, *"Who being the brightness of his glory, and the express image of his person, and upholding all things by the word of his power, when he had by himself purged our sins, sat down on the right hand of the Majesty on high."* Jesus is the very light that radiates off of the Father; he is his express image of his person. That is a little more than just working for the family business. This shows the oneness of the godhead—three but one what a beautiful mystery. Jesus said if you have seen him you have seen the Father. We need to be a reflection of Christ, so that when they see us they see Jesus. Ministry can be defined in one verse.

"To whom God would make known what is the riches of the glory of this mystery among the Gentiles; which is Christ in you, the hope of glory." (Colossians 1:27)

Real Kingdom ministry puts Jesus on display. From Luke 2:49 to John 14:9, we see a progressive revelation of who Jesus always was. It was progressive to the world around him, but he always was who he was. Jesus himself said, *"Before Abraham was I am."* As we look at the revealing of a maturity process in Christ we must understand that we mature as we walk with him. We walk with him by hearing what he says and obeying. We don't walk with God on our terms, but rather on his terms because he is the Lord.

Remembering the foundational truth of the Christian faith and of Kingdom theology, we must remember that Christ is supreme and above his name there is none. Jesus was fully God and also fully man. I repeat this continually because of its importance and profound affect on our heart and mind. When we remember who Jesus really is we are filled with faith, hope and love and the greatest of these is love. As a young man Jesus increased in wisdom and stature and in favor with God and man, according to Luke 2:52. As Jesus increased in wisdom and in favor with God and man, his government increased also according to the prophecy from the mouth of Isaiah, see Isaiah 9:6. If Jesus who was God in the flesh had to increase in wisdom and in favor with God and man, how much more do we as humans? Increase always speaks of inheritance. Without a consistent increase there is no room for an inheritance. All because of what Jesus has done we are adopted. Jesus ransomed us back to God with his very own blood. One of the most foundational truths is simply that we belong to Jesus because of the shedding of his blood. Through the offering up of his Spirit we receive the Spirit of Adoption and are translated from the Kingdom of darkness unto the Kingdom of God's dear and beloved Son Jesus. (Romans 8:15, Ephesians 1:5, Colossians 1:13)

The Kingdom of heaven is the largest adoption agency ever. So we are first adopted. In this time, we learn the cry "Abba, Father." Abba is how a child would relate to his Father and Father is how a mature son would relate to Father. We should never lose the tenderness of heart that cries for Abba, but we should mature so we can be trusted with an inheritance.

"For God so loved the world, that he gave his only begotten Son, that whosoever believeth in him should not perish, but have everlasting life." (John 3:16)

For God so loved the world he gave his son, and for Jesus so loved us he gave us power to become sons. John 1:12 says, *"But as many as received him, to them gave he power to become the sons of God, even to them that believe on his name."* When we receive him, we receive his authority to become who he says we are. The word power used in the verse above literally means authority. Through receiving him we receive authority, which is manifested in our identity before him. As we go from adoption to sonship we mature and our perspectives mature. I will use a natural example to illustrate a spiritual truth. Let's say you adopt a young boy from Africa who is not really familiar with a refrigerator. Before he really gets used to his new family or his new refrigerator, he may be reluctant to use it. However, after he feels comfortable with the family, he will use the refrigerator whenever he pleases. In reality the refrigerator didn't change his mind set about his use of the refrigerator. His mindset changed and then his use of the refrigerator changed. His new family was essential in helping the young boy change his mind. They made him feel at home and he began to behave like himself, or he started to behave like he was truly just another son in his new family. This is a picture or a modern day parable about how Jesus receives us and therefore we receive him and he gives us authority to have access to his resources because we understand we are his children.

As we mature in sonship we in time become ready for our inheritance. We don't earn an inheritance but we grow into a place where we can receive it and then steward it properly with wisdom. The wisdom of God is hidden in a mystery, which means we need revelation from God so that we can possess the wisdom of God. Bill Johnson says it like this, "God doesn't hide things from us; he hides things for us." What I love about revelation is that it's by grace that we receive it. The beauty of inheritance is it's God's grace from one generation to the next. Revelation is God's grace to us and inheritance goes from God to us to others. Inheritances are of grace therefore they are not earned, and even at times not deserved. Similar to the truth that when we were dead in our trespasses we certainly did not deserve Jesus, yet he gave himself for us. One of the things about living in the Kingdom of God is that we live from the merits of Christ Jesus. In modern economic terms we are living from and shopping with his bank account. In religion you will have to earn, but in the Kingdom Jesus paid. Being established in the grace of God is necessary to understand who God has created us to be in him. As much as grace is mentioned we still must understand that grace empowers us to obey God. Grace does not tolerate our disobedient. If you want to see how tolerant God was about sin, look at what Jesus endured on the cross. God is not tolerant or indifferent; he is merciful. Mercy picks us up when we fall and grace empowers us to stand.

Walking with God is the privilege sons and daughters have.

> Romans 8:14-17 says, *"For as many as are led by the Spirit of God, they are the sons of God. For ye have not received the spirit of bondage again to fear; but ye have received the Spirit of adoption, whereby we cry, Abba, Father. The Spirit itself beareth witness with our spirit, that we are the children of God: And if children, then*

> heirs; heirs of God, and joint-heirs with Christ; if so be that we suffer with him, that we may be also glorified together."

Let's see where Paul the Apostle gets this concept.

"And Jesus being full of the Holy Ghost returned from Jordan, and was led by the Spirit into the wilderness." (Luke 4:1)

The concept that the Spirit of God leads sons is rooted in Jesus Christ, God's only begotten Son. All Kingdom theology is seen in Christ, he is the sum of all kingdom equations. Paul continues with his thought and lets us know that the Spirit of Adoption breaks fear and fills our heart with the cry for "Abba, Father." The words "Abba, Father" were only used three places in scripture. Paul used them to share the truth concerning the Spirit of Adoption. The first time it was Christ who used these words in the place of Prayer and the other two times Paul made reference to these same words in Romans 8:15 and Galatians 4:6. Let's see it in Christ to better understand what Paul is saying. Remember what God is saying is rooted in what he has said.

> *"And he went forward a little, and fell on the ground, and prayed that, if it were possible, the hour might pass from him. And he said, Abba, Father, all things are possible unto thee; take away this cup from me: nevertheless not what I will, but what thou wilt."* (Mark 14:35-36)

Here the "Abba" part of his prayer was "if it were possible, the hour might pass from him." The "Father" part of his prayer was "nevertheless not what I want, but what you will." God's will is that we surrender our will and do what he has already revealed to us. Jesus knew exactly what the Father desired. Here the Father was silent and in the Father's silence Jesus heard him. Our inheritance as sons is the mind of Christ. The mind of Christ can hear God when he's silent by remembering what he has said. What is great about the mind of Christ is that it knows the heart of the Father.

However, there is a lesson in this prayer for us. When we don't know his will, we surrender our will and God will reveal to us exactly what he desires. Three quarters of our journey with God is just wholehearted surrender to him. If we aren't willing to surrender, we aren't really willing to be led. Jesus was the perfect example of what a Kingdom life looks like because he lived from the Kingdom toward the situation, circumstances and people. As sons and daughters that is our inheritance. From the place of intercession we move from sonship to inheritance or to being joint-heirs with Christ.

In Luke 15, there is a great story that illustrates something that we just mentioned. First let's start by establishing something. Luke 15 has three parables. The first parable is about a shepherd seeking a lost sheep, see Luke 15:1-7. This parable releases a revelation of the Lord Jesus Christ. The second parable in Luke 15:8-10 was about a woman who lost a coin in her house and a candle is lit so she can find her lost coin. This parable reveals God the Holy Spirit who searches. The third parable is often called the parable of the prodigal son. However, the scriptures don't say that. This parable actually more accurately should be called the parable of the Good Father. This parable illustrates many things but primarily it reveals the nature and character of God the Father. So the younger gets an inheritance before he is ready to steward it wisely. Sometimes we should just be happy when God doesn't just give us what we are asking for. The younger son or the prodigal son goes and spends him money on sin. Just remember sin is expensive, it cost this man his inheritance and Jesus his life. So he finally comes to himself and returns home. His father sees him and runs out to meet him, which is good news. Anyway the father throws a party for his younger son who returned home. This causes the older son to be jealous. There is some truth in here that I believe is necessary to see.

> *"And he was angry, and would not go in: therefore came his father out, and entreated him. And he answering said to his father, Lo, these many years do I serve thee, neither transgressed I at any time thy commandment:*

> and yet thou never gavest me a kid, that I might make merry with my friends: But as soon as this thy son was come, which hath devoured thy living with harlots, thou hast killed for him the fatted calf. And he said unto him, Son, thou art ever with me, and all that I have is thine." (Luke 15:28-31)

The older son lived with the Father but didn't really know him. Mel Tari author of "Like a Mighty Wind" said it like this, "He lived in the Father's house but did not have the Father's heart." He didn't know his Father heart, which overflowed into him not knowing all that the father had was his. Being a joint-heir means all that the owner has we have. Paul mentioned being a joint-heir with Christ. Here the older son did not know the Father's heart; he didn't know that he was a joint-heir, and he lived with everything around him being his but never knew it. The older brother didn't understand sonship and so he never knew what was truly his. This parable is loaded with revelation. It's important to know the Father's heart and steward an inheritance with wisdom. Learning from other people's mistake makes us wise. While learning from our own mistakes makes us just like everyone else. Sonship should lead to inheritance, which should be a wise stewardship of revelation, resources and relationships. In the kingdom, everyone has an inheritance. In the Kingdom, there are no slaves or servants just sons and daughters who lead and steward the inheritance of our Father by serving just like our big brother Jesus.

> Revelation 1:4-6 says, *"John to the seven churches which are in Asia: Grace be unto you, and peace, from him which is, and which was, and which is to come; and from the seven Spirits which are before his throne; And from Jesus Christ, who is the faithful witness, and the first begotten of the dead, and the prince of the kings of the earth. Unto him that loved us, and washed us from our sins in his own blood, And hath made us kings and priests unto God and his Father; to him be glory and dominion for ever and ever. Amen."*

The blood of Jesus makes us who we are. Paul said it like this, "I am who I am by the grace of God." The grace of God that is towards us is the blood of Jesus that speaks a better word for us. His blood doesn't just speak and save but it creates. It turns sinners into Kings and Priests. Being a King or Priest in the days that the book of Revelation was written generally meant that you inherited the priesthood of the Kingdom that your Father ruled in. In the Old Testament, you couldn't go to Bible school to be a priest. Either one was born into the Levitical priesthood or not. Often that was the case with Kings also. We have a very rich heritage in the Lord Jesus Christ. He is the high priest of our profession and also the King of Kings. His blood has made us Kings, which makes him the King of Kings because he is our King.

> *"And I saw heaven opened, and behold a white horse; and he that sat upon him was called Faithful and True, and in righteousness he doth judge and make war. His eyes were as a flame of fire, and on his head were many crowns; and he had a name written, that no man knew, but he himself. And he was clothed with a vesture dipped in blood: and his name is called The Word of God. And the armies which were in heaven followed him upon white horses, clothed in fine linen, white and clean. And out of his mouth goeth a sharp sword, that with it he should smite the nations: and he shall rule them with a rod of iron: and he treadeth the winepress of the fierceness and wrath of Almighty God. And he hath on his vesture and on his thigh a name written, KING OF KINGS, AND LORD OF LORDS."* (Revelation 19:11-16)

This is the greatest picture of the Supremacy of Christ; one crown is not enough for him. He is crowned with many crowns because he is the King of Kings. One crown is simply not enough for all that he is. I must confess to you that I absolutely love this man Jesus.

We have an inheritance in Christ that is beyond words. However, I hope to by the grace of God try to briefly communicate the inheritance and the responsibilities that come with the privileges we have been given through Jesus. We have been made kings and priests. The main characteristic of a priest is humility before God and the main characteristic of a King is authority before men. Here there is something we must understand about the heavenly calling that is in Christ Jesus; we must be humble enough to use the authority Jesus gave us. The measure of humility we maintain on the inside is the amount of sustainable authority we can walk in. Our humility will determine if we can be trusted with Kingdom authority. The authority we receive from God is directly connected to how much of our lives we surrender to God. A priest's main influence is in the heavens through the intercession of incense. Meaning the incense of the Old Testament was a picture of intercession. A King's main influence is in his geographical region in where his Kingdom is. We have a religious and political responsibility whether we like it or not. Often when reading the Bible we don't realize that Jesus had more political names than religious names. For example here are some of his religions names, Teacher or Rabbi, Shepard, High Priest, and Bishop of our souls. Here are some of his Political names, Lord of Hosts, King of Kings, Lord of Lords, Prince of Peace, Man of War, Son of David, Messiah, Apostle and Governor of the Nations. If our policies don't line up with righteousness and justice, which is the foundation of his throne they simply are not Kingdom. The kingdom has to trump our tradition or preferences. We as blood bought sons and daughters must be more about our Father's business and interests than our racial, political, personal or even national interests. What I am saying is Jesus must really be Lord over our life both doctrinally, experientially, socially, politically, financially and relationally. As priests we serve, as kings we rule and a kingdom of priests rules by serving. Jesus' on earth as it is in heaven prayer is answered in us when we hear him and obey him. Priests are to influence the heavens in the place of intercession, and kings are to influence the earth through their acts of obedience. In the Kingdom all leadership is expressed through service.

CHAPTER 15

KINGDOM PROMOTION

True promotion is simply forward motion. In the Kingdom of God there is only one direction and that is forward. Philippians 3:13-14 says, *"Brethren, I count not myself to have apprehended: but this one thing I do, forgetting those things which are behind, and reaching forth unto those things which are before, I press toward the mark for the prize of the high calling of God in Christ Jesus."* To press forward we must look ahead and forget what is behind us. Often the past is holding us back from God's future. When we learn to see what God is doing, we can be led by the Spirit and move forward with the Kingdom. Part of seeing in the Spirit is just obeying God's written word and choosing not to walk after the flesh or its lusts. Promotion comes to us when we learn to do what God is doing and say what God is saying. If the Kingdom of God is marching forward from eternity past into time and space now with many prophecies yet to be fulfilled, it is safe to say that the Kingdom is moving forward and it cannot be stopped. If the Kingdom is moving forward and we are not moving with it we are backslidden. The way people fall away from the faith is simply when they stop moving forward. Unfortunately, I have watched people fall away and I want to share with you the pattern that I have consistently seen. The Kingdom is moving forward and Jesus is requiring something of them and they say no similar to the rich young ruler who loved his money more than God, Luke 18:22-25. Often falling away happens something like this. Someone fails to be accountable to others, then they stop fellowshipping with other believers and before you know it they are no longer in an authentic relationship with Jesus or the body of Christ. A relationship with Jesus on our terms is no relationship at all. Many times one falls away from the body of Christ before one falls away from the head. The opposite of moving forward is falling away.

However, I know you desire to move forward with Jesus and his coming Kingdom that is here and still coming. New Jerusalem has not reigned down from above and so the Kingdom is still coming because it is ever increasing. Some say it like this "the Kingdom now but not yet." I would word it more like this, "The Kingdom is here now, and it's coming." in the words or Randy Clark "there is more!" However the pursuit of more should never cause us to neglect what we have already be given. We live in the more of God because his Kingdom is increasing. God gave me some keys to move forward in his Kingdom, and I want to share them with you. The still small voice of the Holy Spirit took over my renewed mind and said, "I want to give you three keys to moving forward with the Kingdom." He then said, "purity, humility and excellence." There are others and I will share them as well. But first I want to share that this invitation by Holy Spirit wasn't just an invitation to success of performance; it was an invitation to intimately and obediently walk with him and in that process he is going to make me like Christ. The Kingdom of God is the only Kingdom where everything the King does and says is in the best interests of his royal citizens, who were made Kings and Priests by the shedding of his very own blood. The goal of the king is to make his citizens just like him.

Purity is one of God's number one priorities, which is why God allows the pure in heart to see him. If our heart is pure we can see God, if our hands are clean we can participate with him in what he is doing in the earth today. David had "bloody hands" and so he could not build the temple of God. I am not preaching performance although we will be judged according to our works. However, I am speaking about a love for God that causes us to obey him so his Kingdom is manifested through our lives of purity. I love my wife; she's amazing. The most amazing thing about her is she is only my wife, and I don't share her with another. The church must get out of bed with the world especially if we want to see the Kingdom come to our cities. If you think what I am saying is far-fetched see Revelation 2-3. The Kingdom of God will only facilitate a marriage between Christ and a pure and spotless bride. The Father simply won't have it any other way. Here is a verse that clearly shows how God honors the decision to be pure.

> *"But Daniel purposed in his heart that he would not defile himself with the portion of the king's meat, nor with the wine which he drank: therefore he requested of the prince of the eunuchs that he might not defile himself. Now God had brought Daniel into favor and tender love with the prince of the eunuchs."* (Daniel 1:8-9)

Daniel made a choice on the inside that affected what God did on the outside. We must choose to be pure, and God will bring us into favor and give us grace and strength to walk out our decision. Purity is a one-time choice and an everyday decision.

Humility is before honor, according to the wisest human ever to live. 1 Peter 5:5-6 says, *"Likewise, ye younger, submit yourselves unto the elder. Yea, all of you be subject one to another, and be clothed with humility: for God resisteth the proud, and giveth grace to the humble. Humble yourselves therefore under the mighty hand of God, that he may exalt you in due time."* God gives grace or favor to the humble and resists the proud. If we are going to move forward with God, we are going to have to "walk humbly with our God." We are not only to walk humbly; we are to be clothed with humility. If you are humble then in due time you should walk in favor and be put into a role where you can deeply influence others so the

Kingdom can advance and the name of Jesus can be glorified. If we are not being lifted up, how humble are we really? Being humble is not about being quiet, or having a feminine tone of voice, or not being confrontational. Humility is seen clearly in that we simply obey God no matter how we or the world around us thinks or feels about it. The disciples were not too thrilled about Jesus' death, but it pleased the Father to bruise him. Sometimes the most sincere believers don't perceive what God is doing.

> *"And being found in fashion as a man, he humbled himself, and became obedient unto death, even the death of the cross. Wherefore God also hath highly exalted him, and given him a name which is above every name: That at the name of Jesus every knee should bow, of things in heaven, and things in earth, and things under the earth; And that every tongue should confess that Jesus Christ is Lord, to the glory of God the Father."* (Philippians 2:8-11)

Jesus humbled himself and became obedient to the death of a cross and now he is highly exalted with a name above all names. Just as Peter said that if you humble yourself God will exalt you. God will not exalt us to be worshipped, but God will exalt us to a place of high influence so we can serve the Kingdom in a place of authority. God's favor on someone is his way of honoring that person. Humility is before honor, but true humility will lead to honor. Honor is another key in the Kingdom to promotion. The test of authentic honor is not how we treat people who are superior in our workplace or at church. True honor is seen in how we treat people who have less authority, less influence, and less money than us.

"He that oppresseth the poor reproacheth his Maker: but he that honoureth him hath mercy on the poor." (Proverbs 14:31)

Our honor for King Jesus is seen in our mercy for the poor. The connection between our love for God and our care for humanity is inseparable Biblically speaking. When we are truly humble our first thoughts are not "how will brother I have a concern" feel but rather how does Jesus feel about this. Kingdom people are not influenced by the outside world. They live from the Christ within who sits on the throne of their hearts and tells them how they should feel, speak and act. Humility is a key to promotion in the same way that humility is the key to being honored and exalted.

Often when we think of humility we think poverty. Sometimes poor people are humble but at other times that is simply not true. Humility of heart is simply the dependency of mind, or the deep acknowledgement of one's need for God at all times in all circumstances no matter what. Here are a few verses that show us we can have a highly exalted seat and have a low hear of great humility.

> "And I beheld, and, lo, in the midst of the throne and of the four beasts, and in the midst of the elders, stood a Lamb as it had been slain, having seven horns and seven eyes, which are the seven Spirits of God sent forth into all the earth. And he came and took the book out of the right hand of him that sat upon the throne. And when he had taken the book, the four beasts and four and twenty elders fell down before the Lamb, having every one of them harps, and golden vials full of odours, which are the prayers of saints. And they sung a new song, saying, Thou art worthy to take the book, and to open the seals thereof: for thou wast slain, and hast redeemed us to God by thy blood out of every kindred, and tongue, and people, and nation; And hast made us unto our God kings and priests: and we shall reign on the earth." (Revelation 5:6-10)

The twenty-four elders have the highest seat of honor in the entire universe. They surround the creator and sustainer of all things. The elders literally encircle the Ancient of Days, the very Lamb of God. They have a high seat but a low heart. When one's chest is on the floor it's because he or she has a humble heart. The elders willingly throw themselves off of their seat of honor to worship the

Lamb who was slain, who humbled himself to the death of a cross. Let me say it a little more clearly. Jesus means more to them than their position or title.

Excellence is a true virtue of the Kingdom because everything in the Kingdom reflects the King. Here are several verses that make this truth more visible.

• Job 37:23 *"Touching the Almighty, we cannot find him out: he is excellent in power, and in judgment, and in plenty of justice: he will not afflict."* Here we see that he is excellent in power, judgment and justice because he will not afflict or he is merciful.

• Psalm 8:9 *"O LORD our Lord, how excellent is thy name in all the earth!"* The word name here in Hebrew is referencing his Character and Authority. So by saying his name is excellent that means excellent is who he is. Therefore, what he does is excellent. Character is who we are and authority is what we do.

• Psalm 16:3 *"But to the saints that are in the earth, and to the excellent, in whom is all my delight."* I personally love this verse because here we see "excellent" as a person in who all of God's delight fits in. This is none other than Christ the Lord. As people of the Kingdom we are supposed to reflect Christ, and he is excellent; therefore, everything we do must be marked by excellence if it's going to have the signature of Jesus upon it. Excellence is all we do that causes people to pay attention to the words we speak. Another very similar example would be if people don't see our integrity, they will not want to hear our truth. In order for Kingdom promotion to be sustainable, integrity is an absolute must.

Here are a few stories of excellence in motion. Everything in the Kingdom is excellent to say the least. 1 Kings 10:3-10 says, "And Solomon told her all her questions: there was not any thing hid from the king, which he told her not. And when the queen of Sheba had seen all Solomon's wisdom, and the house that he had built, And the meat of his table, and the sitting of his servants, and the attendance of his ministers, and their apparel, and his cupbearers, and his ascent by which he went up unto the house of the LORD; there was no more spirit in her. And she said to the king, It was a true report that I heard in mine own land of thy acts and of thy wisdom. Howbeit I believed not the words, until I came, and mine eyes had seen it: and, behold, the half was not told me: thy wisdom and prosperity exceedeth the fame which I heard. Happy are thy men, happy are these thy servants, which stand continually before thee, and that hear thy wisdom. Blessed be the LORD thy God, which delighted in thee, to set thee on the throne of Israel: because the LORD loved Israel for ever, therefore made he thee king, to do judgment and justice. And she gave the king an hundred and twenty talents of gold, and of spices very great store, and precious stones: there came no more such abundance of spices as these which the queen of Sheba gave to king Solomon." Solomon had wisdom, which caused heathens to listen. There was nothing he couldn't answer. His wisdom on the inside was reflected by everything he did on the outside. The queen of Sheba was at a loss for breath over seemingly natural things such as an amazing house, the meat of his table, the sitting of his servants, how his servants served, their clothing, his cupbearers and his ascent from his house to God's. One of the fruits of wisdom and understanding is excellence. Someone who is of an excellent spirit places value on the little things that other people overlook, which is why they may stand out in a crowd. In the world we live in excellence is huge, it actually gives us the right to speak to people who normally wouldn't listen to us.

"He that hath knowledge spareth his words: and a man of understanding is of an excellent spirit." (Proverbs 17:27)

Through Solomon's wisdom, excellence was reflected in everything he said, did and in everything that surrounded him. It was Solomon's wisdom that was of course given by God's grace that caused the queen of Sheba to have a powerful revelation. She said this to Solomon, *"Blessed be the Lord thy God, which delighted in thee, to set thee on the throne of Israel: because the Lord loved Israel forever, therefore made he thee king, to do righteousness and justice."* The queen of Sheba has a bit of revelation about several profound things.

She began by blessing the Lord and saying that God delighted in Solomon and that is why he is on the throne. Here we see that God gives authority to those he delights in. She also mentions that God is making Solomon do what is right because of his everlasting love for his chosen people Israel. She gets revelation on God's feelings for Solomon and his everlasting love for his people all because of Solomon's wisdom and excellence. The wisdom which, produced excellence was the grace of God. So the grace that was put upon him revealed the heart of the God who gave Solomon the grace or gift of wisdom and understanding. It's fair to say that Solomon *"let his light so shine before men,"* that the queen of Sheba knew the heart of God because of his wisdom in action, which was manifested in excellence. When we use what God has given us or simply do what he tells us others come into contact with him.

Daniel was another man of excellence.

> Daniel 5:11-14 says, *"There is a man in thy kingdom, in whom is the spirit of the holy gods; and in the days of thy father light and understanding and wisdom, like the wisdom of the gods, was found in him; whom the king Nebuchadnezzar thy father, the king, I say, thy father, made master of the magicians, astrologers, Chaldeans, and soothsayers; Forasmuch as an excellent spirit, and knowledge, and understanding, interpreting of dreams, and showing of hard sentences, and dissolving of doubts, were found in the same Daniel, whom the king named Belteshazzar: now let Daniel be called, and he will show the interpretation. Then was Daniel brought in before the king. And the king spake and said unto Daniel, Art thou that Daniel, which art of the children of the captivity of Judah, whom the king my father brought out of Jewry? I have even heard of thee, that the spirit of the gods is in thee, and that light and understanding and excellent wisdom is found in thee."*

Here an excellent Spirit was in Daniel, which caused doubt to be dissolved in those around Daniel. We know this excellent Spirit is

Mr. Holy Spirit himself. Remember he does all things well. Daniel didn't just have wisdom; he had excellent wisdom, which means he knew what they didn't because of the God who lived inside of him. Excellence leads to promotion.

> *"Then this Daniel was preferred above the presidents and princes, because an excellent spirit was in him; and the king thought to set him over the whole realm."* (Daniel 6:3)

The other princes and presidents became jealous of Daniel because the King was going to give him authority over the whole realm. Real favor will produce jealousy in those who do not guard their hearts. True favor will produce jealousy just like the story of Joseph the dreamer and his jealous brothers who sold him into slavery. Here is a little bit of wisdom, don't tell your dreams to half brothers because it will often produce jealousy. If we continue with Daniel's story, God rescues him from the "power of the lion" and he comes out un-harmed. What the enemy planned for evil God turned to the "good news of the Kingdom" went out into all the earth through the royal decree of a heathen king, see Daniel 6:24-28.

> *"Promotion comes to us as we move forward with God and one another. Love is the more excellent way of the Kingdom. Promotion is not our business but it's God's business to those who are faithful. For promotion cometh neither from the east, nor from the west, nor from the south. But God is the judge: he putteth down one, and setteth up another."* (Psalm 75:6-7)

Promotion comes because God rewards those who diligently seek him. God rewards us publicly for what we do privately. When we go after God and make his business our business, he makes our business his business. Another simple key to moving forward in the Kingdom is to begin to see what God is doing and partner with him. To keep it simpler, in order to speak to our understanding John the beloved revelator said it like this.

Adam LiVecchi

"He that committeth sin is of the devil; for the devil sinneth from the beginning. For this purpose the Son of God was manifested, that he might destroy the works of the devil." (1 John 3:8)

The works of the devil are many and they are usually fairly easy to see and discern if we are willing to care and look. The Kingdom of God is moving forward displacing the darkness through the light of the glorious Gospel. Where there is sickness, we are to bring healing in Jesus' name. Where there are people damned to hell all around us we are to bring a demonstration of who Jesus is with our words, actions and with power when needed. Where there is the demonic, we are supposed to bring deliverance. Where there is no clean drinking water, we are to bring clean drinking water. Where there are no churches, we are supposed to plant churches. Where babies are being slaughtered, we are supposed to be a voice for those with no voice. Where the orphan and widow are crying our shoulders are to be where their tears fall. Where there is prostitution and child slave labor, when the undocumented person is getting financially taken advantage of in our local restaurants we need to stand up and speak out. I think you may be getting the point. Where there is prayerlessness in the church, we are supposed to establish night and day prayer. Where there is spiritual blindness and complacency, we are supposed to bring a vision and a hope filled, love motivated strategy that makes room for others to walk with Jesus and move forward in the Kingdom. If we are going to move forward in the Kingdom, we need to have the heart and mind of the King as well as his priorities. His priorities will awaken passion that will open the door to compassion, which should then cause us to take action.

CHAPTER 16

THE ATTRIBUTES OF THE KINGDOM

This chapter can be written because to you it has been given to know the mysteries of the Kingdom. Matthew 13:11 says, "He answered and said unto them, Because it is given unto you to know the mysteries of the kingdom of heaven, but to them it is not given." When Paul was writing to the Corinthians, he mentioned the mysteries of God. Perhaps Paul's concept is rooted in what Jesus had previously said. Remember what God is saying is rooted in what he has said. Often what God has said is the springboard for what he is saying.

"Let a man so account of us, as of the ministers of Christ, and stewards of the mysteries of God. Moreover it is required in stewards, that a man be found faithful." (1 Corinthians 4:1)

The key to more in the Kingdom is not asking for more, but being faithful with what we have already received freely. Ministers are supposed to possess several kinds of mysteries.

> *"It is the glory of God to conceal a thing: but the honor of kings is to search out a matter."* (Proverbs 25:2)

God's glory is imparted as a mystery is revealed. Because the Kingdom of God is ever increasing, revelation will eternally be unfolded. The most amazing part of this is Jesus never changes, so it will take more than forever for him to be fully revealed. If that doesn't get you happy or teary eyed, check your pulse.

God expresses love many ways but one of them is revelation.

> John 5:19-20 says, *"Then answered Jesus and said unto them, Verily, verily, I say unto you, The Son can do nothing of himself, but what he seeth the Father do: for what things soever he doeth, these also doeth the Son likewise. For the Father loveth the Son, and showeth him all things that himself doeth: and he will show him greater works than these, that ye may marvel."*

Here Jesus was receiving revelation from his Father and he understood it to be the Father's love that showed him what to do. The revelation that Jesus is speaking about is revelation that leads to action. The Kingdom is eternally increasing and so action on our part is necessary if we are going to keep partnering with the King and his Kingdom. Often when we think of being backslidden we think of someone who stops reading their Bible or coming to church. That is partially true, but being backslidden also can mean that one stops moving forward with God for Kingdom purposes. Remember consistent obedience to the King manifests and establishes his Kingdom on earth as it is in heaven. Our obedience should not be performance driven; it should be love driven. It should be a reflection of our love for him, which is only really possible because he first loved us. The revelation that we receive from God is him actually saying, "I really love you and I want to show you how to walk with and partner with me." So think of the rest of this chapter as God's love for you because he has good plans for you. The Father loved so he gave Jesus and adopted us. Jesus came and gave the mysteries of the Kingdom to son's and daughter's. He ascended on high and poured out the Holy Spirit so we can never be alone and bring the world back to the Father's house so that his big house with many mansions would be full. Jesus was poured out so his Father's house could be full; it means that much to the Father. You mean that much to him.

Narrow is the way and straight is the gate that leads to life, and few find it. I believe you are part of that few that found it. I also believe few to God is different than our "few" similar to a day to God is as a thousands years. The narrow way and the straight gate is the road to the cross because in the Kingdom to live you must die. The kingdom of God operates differently from the Kingdom of men; I will explain that in my final thoughts in a more detailed way. Not only is the cross the draw bridge into the Kingdom, but also Jesus himself is the door.

"Then said Jesus unto them again, Verily, verily, I say unto you, I am the door of the sheep." (John 10:7)

Jesus is the only entrance into the Kingdom. It's either through the veil of his flesh, which is the door or it's no way at all. What is amazing about the message of the Kingdom is that Jesus preached it, but also that it begins to reveal all that he is. To know the most about someone you must go to their home. Their true values are more clearly reflected there. Jesus was the express image of the Father, but the more he reveals his Kingdom to us the more we get to know him and his ways. The Kingdom is the perfect atmosphere to reveal the King and all of his glory. If we are going to pray fervently "On earth as it is in heaven" perhaps we should know more about heaven.

The economy and currency of heaven. Heaven has an economy and a currency and we should understand it so we can have access to it here on earth. The Lord of the economy is Christ; all authority from the Father has been entrusted to him.

"And I will shake all nations, and the desire of all nations shall come: and I will fill this house with glory, saith the LORD of hosts. The silver

is mine, and the gold is mine, saith the LORD of hosts." (Haggai 2:7-8)

While the nations are being shaken, the glory is on the way and the Lord is fully in charge of the economy. When the Lord says the silver and the gold belong to him, perhaps he is giving an investment tip? On January 12, 2010, I was in Haiti when God himself shook it, as he mentioned he would in Haggai 2 and in Matthew 24. There were 100,000 dead peoples in the city, and I was in during the quake. In the midst of shaking, we have received a "Kingdom that does not shake." In fact it's unshakable because our King is the one doing the shaking! Shaking makes way for glory and the one who shakes sends the glory and holds the economy in his hands. We have access to the Kingdom by grace, but all transactions are through faith. Faith is the currency of the Kingdom. If you read Hebrews 11, often known as the Faith chapter, faith always seemed to be doing something. Faith naturally brings about supernatural things because it is the currency from above. In the Kingdom, there is a lot to understand about investment but there are two I will mention. The first is if we want to invest in the King and his Kingdom it happens as we give to the poor. Giving to the poor is actually lending to the Lord. That is a pretty wise investment. Continuing with the same concept, Jesus told the rich young ruler to give all that he had to the poor and to come follow him. It's pretty interesting how giving to the poor and following Jesus is in the very same breath. When Jesus showed up to Zacchaeus' house, he immediately gave half of his possessions to the poor. Again the association with Jesus and the poor is almost inseparable. Another wise investment is people and not merely religious structures or nice church buildings. In Luke 19, there is a parable where a nobleman gives money to three servants. Two are faithful and one ends up in hell. Here we can see that the Kingdom invests in people. God entrusts people naturally so he can later entrust them spiritually. Faithful stewardship which actually includes wisdom and risk resulted in them being entrusted with cities. Their natural faithfulness was a key to an increase of their spiritual authority in the Kingdom. Transactions in the Kingdom are by faith and through faithfulness authority and influence increase because God rewards the diligent and faithful.

The Increase of His Government

Jesus sells gold from the Kingdom to the church. Here Jesus is talking to Laodicea.

> *"I know thy works, that thou art neither cold nor hot: I would thou wert cold or hot. So then because thou art lukewarm, and neither cold nor hot, I will spue thee out of my mouth. Because thou sayest, I am rich, and increased with goods, and have need of nothing; and knowest not that thou art wretched, and miserable, and poor, and blind, and naked: I counsel thee to buy of me gold tried in the fire, that thou mayest be rich; and white raiment, that thou mayest be clothed, and that the shame of thy nakedness do not appear; and anoint thine eyes with eyesalve, that thou mayest see. As many as I love, I rebuke and chasten: be zealous therefore, and repent. Behold, I stand at the door, and knock: if any man hear my voice, and open the door, I will come in to him, and will sup with him, and he with me. To him that overcometh will I grant to sit with me in my throne, even as I also overcame, and am set down with my Father in his throne. He that hath an ear, let him hear what the Spirit saith unto the churches."* (Revelation 3:15-22)

There's a lot here but one thing we can learn is that Jesus is the only gold salesman who wants to make those he is selling gold to rich. All others salesmen are tying to make themselves rich off you but he is trying to make us rich off himself. This too is good news. What's interesting about this church is that their works were a reflection of their true poverty even though they thought they were rich. I would call that deceived, how about you? What about us? Sometimes we have to ask ourselves hard questions if we really want to move forward with the Kingdom. Their inward condition was outwardly manifested in their lack of works, which meant they were actually lukewarm. True zeal is repenting or changing the way we think which should change the way we live and even what we live for.

The atmosphere of the Kingdom. Often atmosphere and economy have something to do with one another. In areas where poverty is everywhere often one may feel danger in that place. However, in an affluent area one may tend to feel less danger. In the Kingdom of Heaven, there is no lack so peace and joy are the atmosphere. The atmosphere is peace and joy because God is there, and because he is ruling from heaven there is no lack. The Kingdom of God is righteousness, peace, and joy in the Holy Spirit. Jesus' righteousness was given or imputed to us and by faith we receive it. This means we have peace towards God. When this reality touches our heart and Spirit, joy is the only result. The joy may come with tears, but nevertheless its joy unspeakable and so sometimes tears speak of the unspeakable to God. Tears are valuable to God, so much that he bottles them. I personally think that the rain over our lives may sometimes be the brokenness of our hearts.

The King communicates many ways but has one language and it's not English; it's truth in every possible dialect for its many difference citizens who are advancing the Kingdom in their different cultures here on planet earth. The language of the Kingdom is truth. Jesus is the truth and so one of his limitations is that he can't lie. In the kingdom of God, there is no deception, no fear of deception, and no false doctrines. Everything is certain in the Kingdom. Remember it does not shake; there are no recessions in the Kingdom. What Jesus says he means. There is no hypocrisy in the Kingdom of Heaven. Hypocrisy is saying one thing and doing another. The reason we can put our trust in Jesus and his leadership is because he is not a hypocrite. Religion is merely a reflection of something that just isn't Christ. Religion can appear like Christ but not have the power that Christ has to change lives and the world around us. The truth is the verbalized certainty of the atmosphere in heaven invading the uncertainties of earth. Truth is the communication of a person (Christ Jesus) who determines the atmosphere anywhere he goes. When Jesus spoke peace to the storm then his peace or Kingdom came upon that storm and that was the truth. The facts were there was a storm. The truth was that when Jesus spoke to it his Kingdom atmosphere came upon it and overtook it because he is supreme. In times of great uncertainty a hunger for truth is emerging and will be demonstrated by a people who love Jesus enough to obey him and manifest the Kingdom through godly character, acts of power and great wisdom to make it sustainable and available to the most vulnerable on this planet. The greater the uncertainties of our day the deeper the hunger for truth will become. God is setting the stage for us to have the solutions this planet needs. Those solutions are found in Jesus and received from him who is the wisdom and power of God.

The architecture of the Kingdom reveals the nature of the King. Everything in the Kingdom of God is eternally excellent.

"Jesus answered and said unto him, Verily, verily, I say unto thee, Except a man be born again, he cannot see the kingdom of God." (John 3:3)

We are born from above to live seated with Christ in heavenly places and not just to merely go to church on Sunday. I find this very interesting especially when the walls of the Kingdom are called salvation.

"Violence shall no more be heard in thy land, wasting nor destruction within thy borders; but thou shalt call thy walls Salvation, and thy gates Praise." (Isaiah 60:18)

The gates of the Kingdom are called praise. Gates speak of authority; kingdom authority is released through praise because God comes to inhabit the praises of his people.

The Kingdom of heaven has widows and this is really good for the earth. On the earth when a window is open it could be good for fresh air but also bugs can get in. However, in the Kingdom when the windows are opened it is so God can pour out a blessing.

"Bring ye all the tithes into the storehouse, that there may be meat in mine house, and prove me now herewith, saith the LORD of hosts, if I will not open you the windows of heaven, and pour you out a blessing, that there shall not be room enough to receive it. And

> *I will rebuke the devourer for your sakes, and he shall not destroy the fruits of your ground; neither shall your vine cast her fruit before the time in the field, saith the LORD of hosts."* (Malachi 3:10-11)

Not only does heaven come down when God opens his windows, but hell is pushed back on earth. When the Kingdom comes, hell is displaced.

The agriculture in the Kingdom is completely supernatural. In the developing, world millions upon millions of people drink from wells. The results are less than salvation. As a matter of fact, half of the people on this planet are in hospital beds due to unsafe drinking water. The wells in the kingdom are called "the wells of salvation." There is a river in the kingdom that flows from the King himself.

> *"And he showed me a pure river of water of life, clear as crystal, proceeding out of the throne of God and of the Lamb. In the midst of the street of it, and on either side of the river, was there the tree of life, which bare twelve manner of fruits, and yielded her fruit every month: and the leaves of the tree were for the healing of the nations."* (Revelation 22:1-2)

This river literally flows from the wounded side of the Lamb. That eternal fountain was opened on Calvary and never stopped flowing. From the wounded side of the Lamb, the water literally causes the tree of life to produce leave that literally bring healing to the nations. The same tree produces twelve different kinds of fruit all year around. In the kingdom fruitfulness is the only option. From death life flows. When we live in the Kingdom, we can be fruitful in every season. This is supernatural for several reasons. The first reason is where the water comes from. The second reason is that the tree always bears fruit and the third is that different fruit comes from the same tree. The agriculture and the culture of the Kingdom are completely supernatural.

The Increase of His Government

The scepter in the Kingdom is called righteousness. The throne is called grace; the foundations of it are righteousness and justice and the seat is mercy. The throne has wheels and moves. The throne is on a sea of glass. Usually chairs don't just sit on water without sinking. There is nothing usual or natural about the Kingdom of God; it is above the natural. The name of Jesus is the strong tower in the Kingdom. As citizens from above, we should learn more about home; we should store up treasure in heaven. We should set our affections on the things above. Our citizenship should be seen in our behavior here on earth. The political scope of the Kingdom is a sovereign monarchy; every decision the King makes is in the best interests of his royal blood bought citizens. In the Kingdom, there is freedom.

"Now the Lord is that Spirit: and where the Spirit of the Lord is, there is liberty." (2 Corinthians 3:17)

The Kingdom of God is everlasting because it is ever increasing. Yet the King himself is unchanging.

The Kingdom has roads and paths. There is a narrow way or straight street. The highway in the Kingdom is called holiness, see Isaiah 35:8. The Lesson for earth is that Holiness accelerates destiny; he who has ears to hear let them hear. The paths in the Kingdom are called righteousness. The word "paths" is plural on purpose. There is one way into the Kingdom alone and that is through Jesus the door, but there are many different paths with different purposes once you are in the Kingdom. I will give you an illustration. If Nehemiah didn't drink wine, the wall of Jerusalem would probably have never been rebuilt let alone in 52 days. He was the Kings' cupbearer, so wine was necessary. If Daniel would have drank wine, he would have been defiled according to his own conscience. Here is a small example of the paths of righteousness. It wouldn't have been right for Daniel to drink, and it wouldn't have been right if Nehemiah didn't drink. I am not advocating drinking in the least bit, I am simply illustrating the paths of righteousness are different for different people. Most Christians can't even control their own tongue, so in my opinion liquor is the last thing most believers need. I am not saying if you drink you are going to hell, I am saying if we want to give people Jesus booze is not necessary. Many believers talk about revival, the revivals of the past shut down bars because the fear of the Lord gripped the community, now we have so called revivalist's who throw a few beers back after service. In my opinion we don't need that. Also in the Kingdom we don't need a revival because nothing is dead. What we need is an alignment. We need to align our will and practices with the wisdom of God so people can see Jesus through our lives of surrender. For some people being a missionary is a must but for others not starting a business is just plain disobedience, which is sin in God's eyes. I know you get the point because you have the mind of Christ. Because you have the mind of Christ you will see the will of God and walk the path of righteousness he has for you.

In the Kingdom of God there is no darkness; the Lamb himself is the light. There is no night because he never stops shining. Perhaps that's why fruit can grow all year around? In the Kingdom there is no Black church or White church or Korean church; there is only one church. It is a blood bought church and everybody wears Jesus. Jesus is the clothing and the fragrance. As a citizen from above, you should know your international anthem. The anthem song of the Kingdom is *"worthy is the Lamb that was slain."* This song must be sung with our lives and not just our lips. As people from above we must bring the Lamb the reward of his suffering. The Lamb has wrath in seven golden vials. He can make gold and fit his wrath in little vials in heaven; truly, there is no one like him. (Revelation 15:7) God can create something that can contain his anger towards all those who reject his Son— wow.

As citizens of the Kingdom, often we feel like square pegs in round holes. Don't feel bad about that feel good about that. That is a proof of your heavenly citizenship. I encourage you to meditate on Jesus and his kingdom. There is room for you in the Father's house; the Father's house has a place just for you. It's a secret place and Jesus himself is the architect. You will love it I am sure. Let all of your confidence be rooted in what Jesus has done for you simply because the Father loved you and was thinking about you before the world was even created. He really likes you, and he's in a good mood. You are a part of his plans; you haven't missed him he's too big. He was with you yesterday, he was with you today and he will be with you tomorrow just trust and obey him and he will manifest and reveal himself to you simply because he said he would In the Kingdom what Jesus says goes, so do what he says and you will have peace that passes understanding no matter the circumstances. Remember peace is bigger and stronger than the storms of this life because Jesus gave the peace and it's yours so hold on to it. He was tortured for it so he really wants you to have it.

FINAL THOUGHTS

MATTHEW 22

Matthew 22: 1-2 says, *"And Jesus answered and spoke unto them again by parables, and said, The kingdom of heaven is like unto a certain king, which made a marriage for his son,"* Here we learn something we should and can never forget. The whole Kingdom of God operates from the Father's love for his Son. It's the Father's desire for Jesus to have a pure and spotless bride that causes the Kingdom to operate. The Father's love for us is what caused him to give Jesus. It's love that motivates the Father, the Son and the Holy Spirit. Love is their bond of unity, and all Kingdom people are motivated or compelled by love. The labor of the Kingdom without love is worthless. Speaking the truth without love is a waste of breath. Love is the more excellent way. Loves gives; it never fails. Love looks like Jesus hanging naked on a tree for you and me. It looks like the Father looking away from Jesus so he would never have to look away from us. After writing this I felt compelled to remind you that, everything operates from the Father's love that is towards us in Christ Jesus. You were created to be loved by God. You were created for his good pleasure. The simplicity of the Kingdom is God loves so he invites and provides for all who come. I hope to see you on that wedding day. That wedding day will be where the Father will walk a bride down the aisle and present a corporate people who are worthy of the blood of his Son. The kingdom of God is the only place with the resources and the environment that is suitable for the grandeur of this great day.

NOTES

NOTES

NOTES

Adam LiVecchi, the leader of We See Jesus Minsitries, lives by faith and has a heart to bring the Word of the Lord to the Body of Christ. His ministry is an itinerant ministry based in Northern NJ. As a result of the Lord's leading he has had the opportunity to minister internationally in Hondorus, China, Mexico, Philippines, India, Peru, Dominican Republic, Brazil, Nicaragua, Haiti, Cuba, Canada, Uraguay, Uganda, Latvia, Estonia and all across the United States.

We See Jesus Ministries seeks to build the Kingdom of God through equipping the local church and delivering the Gospel message with signs and wonders follwing. Adam has the privilege of traveling with his beautiful wife, Sarah, and his brother, Aaron, who are both anointed musicians. Adam is also the co-leader of Voices in the Wilderness School of the Prophets with John Natale. Adam and Sarah LiVecchi look forward to building long lasting relationships that lead to sustainable change for the glory of King Jesus.

We See Jesus Ministries
31 Werneking Place
Little Ferry, NJ 07643
info@weseejesusministries.com
www.WeSeeJesusMinistries.com

Voices in the Wilderness
31 Werneking Place
Little Ferry, NJ 07643
info@voicesinthewilderness.us
www.VoicesintheWilderness.us

MORE BOOKS BY ADAM LIVECCHI

His Name is the Word of God
by Adam LiVecchi

Published by We See Jesus Ministries
Released 2010
Also available in Spanish

So You Want to Change the World?
Authors:
Don Nori Sr., Patricia King, Dee Collins, Rob Coscia, Barbie Breathitt, **Adam LiVecchi**, Abby H. Abildness, Dorsey Marshall, Doug Alexander, Lisa Jo Greer, Susan East, and Jim Wilbur

Published by Destiny Image
Released 2011

The Execution of Jesus Christ
by Adam LiVecchi

Published by We See Jesus Ministries
Released 2011

Available at
www.WeSeeJesusMinistries.com

Sitting at His Feet
Developing Ears to Hear the Voice of Jesus

Soft Cover

Hard Cover

Adam LiVecchi is passionate about Jesus. I say that everytime I hang up the phone with him. There is nothing that stands out as strong as his intense burning desire to see Jesus glorified. I am always refreshed and refocused by spending time listening to him revealate about the Lord. I am excited to be able to stand behind him as his passionate voice is spread far and wide through a new medium, the written word. If Adam is speaking, I am listening, and I recommend that others do the same. Adam's heart desires to see the Body of Christ rise up into the Glorious Bride without spot or wrinkle. Writing from this angle, he takes aim at the heart of the reader and attacks much of what I call *"Churchianity."* It is time to put on the apron, get out the steak sauce and head to the backyard BBQ because there is nothing that Adam likes more than *"Sacred Cows."*

Jonathan Welton
Founder of Jonathan Welton Ministries and Author of School of the Seers and Normal Christianity.
www.JonWelton.com

MANUALS BY ADAM LIVECCHI

Go.Preach.Heal
A practical guide to supernatural living
Ministry Manual by Adam LiVecchi
Released 2011
Released in Portuguese & Spanish 2012

"As I read this latest work from Adam LiVecchi, once again I was challenged by his passion for Jesus. Over the past several years, I have had the opportunity to minister with Adam in a number of developing nations, both working side by side, and recently as he has gone to represent me. Adam's life and ministry are marked by his zeal to preach Christ everywhere he goes. This manual overviews those aspects of the faith that are central in Adam's life. Enjoy, and let Go.Preach.Heal provoke and inspire you."

Steve Stewart
Founder of Impact Nations
Author, When Everything Changes
www.ImpactNations.com

"Go.Preach.Heal: A Practical Guide to Supernatural Living has given us a simple but profound look at what the Christian life should look like. This book is filled with revelation that is beautifully partnered with practical advice on a wide range of everyday issues that helps the reader to live the way Jesus did. This is a wonderful book."

Bill Johnson
Author, When Heaven Invades Earth, and Essential Guide to Healing
Senior Pastor, Bethel Church, Redding, CA
www.iBethel.org

"Adam LiVecchi is a man on a mission to make Jesus famous to a generation that has largely strayed from a life of faith in Christ. The Go.Preach.Heal manual will introduce believers to a gospel of faith in action not mere words. I gladly recommend this manual for anyone wanting to mature in Christ and enter into the supernatural ministry Jesus has entrusted to the saints through the power of the Holy Spirit."

Adam Cates
Senior Pastor of the Big House Church
www.theBigHouseChurch.com

Listen.Learn.Obey
Prophetic Manual
Co-Authored by
John Natale & Adam LiVecchi
Released 2011

Voices in the Wilderness | School of the Prophets
www.VoicesintheWilderness.us

"There are many ministers in the body of Christ that call themselves prophets or prophetic people but haven't been trained in the word or in the sensitivity to hear God's voice. This manual will give those who hunger and thirst to develop an anointing and flow from the Holy Spirit that will mature them to use the prophetic gifts in the market place and in the church. This book is well needed in the body of Christ and I highly recommend it."

Prophet Jim Jorgensen
Sound the Trumpet Ministries International
www.SoundtheTrumpetMinistries.org

"If you hunger to walk in prophetic ministry Listen.Learn.Obey is for you. We have scores of books on prophetic ministry but this is a learners manual. This book puts practical tools in your hand. This book will not be an afternoon read but a seasonal soaking. You will work your way through this book and into a breakthrough. Adam LiVecchi is dedicated to God's own purpose of raising up a prophetic people."

Pastor Alan Hawkins
New Life City Church, Alberqurque, NM
www.NewLifeCity.org

"Adam and Sarah LiVecchi are personal friends of mine, I love them very much and I am honored to endorse Adam's newest book "Listen.Learn.Obey". In Matthew 16:18 Jesus said that the gates of hell would not prevail against the church. It's interesting to point out that gates are not mobile, they do not get up and attack, they are a fixed object. This is because the church is called to advance the Kingdom of Heaven and to live proactively instead of living reactively to the attacks of the enemy. Adam is a man of God who lives life proactively as he follows Jesus and this manual will equip and strengthen the body of Christ in the prophetic so that we can storm the gates of hell in all aspects of society. It's spiritual and practical, simple and yet profound. I highly endorse this manual especially for pastors and leaders who have a desire to be equipped and activated in the prophetic."

Nic Billman
Shores of Grace Ministries
www.ShoresofGrace.com

www.ingramcontent.com/pod-product-compliance
Lightning Source LLC
Chambersburg PA
CBHW052022290426
44112CB00014B/2334